Ages 8 to 88

Fun Skits
About
Bible People

by

V. Louise Cunningham

Cover art by
Jack Kershner

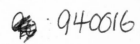 940016

 STANDARD PUBLISHING

Cincinnati, Ohio   14-03355

Dedication

To my loving and wonderful husband who understands me, my children who encourage me, and Mary Lou and her helpful critiquing.

Library of Congress Cataloging-in-Publication Data

Cunningham, V. Louise (Verna Louise), 1933—
    Fun skits about bible people/by V. Louise Cunningham.
        p.   cm.
    ISBN 0-87403-635-6
    1. Bible plays, American. 2. Drama in religious education.
    I. Title.
PS3553.U497F8 1990
812'.54--dc20
                                                89-27305
                                                CIP

Contents

Introduction

As you can see from the cover, this is not serious drama. The skits were written to tickle our imaginations and help us realize Bible people were real people like you and me. While the events are based on Scripture, the dialogue is the author's imagination of the way it could have happened. Each skit does emphasize a main point such as faith, forgiveness, or love.

For any of the skits you can arrange a full-blown production with memorized lines, props, costumes, and scenery, or do a readers theater type of presentation where your characters read their lines. Most of the characters in the skits wear Bible-times clothing. Some modern-day props are used to mix the old with the new.

As you know, material is copyrighted to protect the author and publisher against loss of sales. For some of these skits, however, you would have to buy ten or fifteen copies of the book in order to give all the characters a script. We don't want you to have to do that, so we are hereby giving special permission to copy the skits in this book. For one church to buy a copy of the book and provide another church with copies of a script, or to loan the entire book for that purpose, would of course be an abuse of this special permission.

Have fun with these skits as you learn.

Aboard the USS Ark

Based on Genesis 6-9

This skit is about Noah's faithfulness to God even though he doesn't understand the reason for God's requests. Noah calls a family meeting to tell them God wants him to build an ark. We'll spend time with Noah's family while building the ark and inside the ark once the rain begins. We'll see what life may have been like in close quarters for a long period of time. The skit brings to life Noah and his family and what may have been some of their daily cares and frustrations on board the ark. Maybe Noah and his family had feelings and reactions just as we do. Would we be as trusting as Noah was? Five women, four men and a boy and girl are the characters needed for this skit.

Characters

MOTHER—A mother who tries to bring Bible stories alive for her children. *Christine*

JASON—Her son. *Paul*

SARA—Her daughter. *Mandy*

ZERAH—Noah's daughter-in-law, keeps a diary. ~~Laurie~~ *Lori*

SHEM—Noah's son, married to Zerah. *Matt*

JAPHETH—Noah's son, married to Hannah. *Dan*

HANNAH—Noah's daughter-in-law, always cries. *Christine*

HAM—Noah's son, married to Sarah. ~~Dan~~ ~~Joe~~ *David*

SARAH—Noah's daughter-in-law, practical. ~~Joe~~ *Joe*

NOAH *Rich*

NOAH'S WIFE *Keith*

Props

Mother, her son, and daughter are dressed in modern clothes, the rest of the cast are in Bible-times clothes.

Couch, pillows, vase, small table, dessert, diary, feather pen, clipboard, gangplank, kitchen table and chairs, pots and pans, packing boxes, hankies or tissues, wastebasket to dispose of used hankies or tissues, bird sounds, and stuffed dove are needed.

Scene 1

(Mother, Sara and Jason are sitting on the couch which is located off to one side.)

SARA: Tell us a story, Mother.

JASON: Yes, Mother, tell us a nice long story.

MOTHER: What kind of story would you like to hear?

JASON: One about Noah and the flood.

SARA *(disgusted)*: We know that story. God told Noah to build an ark so he and his family would be saved.

MOTHER: How about one of our "could it be stories" about the flood?

JASON: That's all right with me.

SARA: You mean a pretend story, right?

MOTHER: Something like that. Let's see. God spoke to Noah and told him how to build an ark. The Bible doesn't tell us anything about his sons and their wives. We don't even know the names of Noah's wife or his daughters-in-law. I think Zerah would be a good name for the main character in our story. Can you think of two other names?

JASON: I know, how about Mary?

SARA: That's New Testament. How about Sarah?

JASON: Of course, you'd think of that. How about Samuel's mother? What was her name?

MOTHER: Hannah. Should we use Hannah and Sarah?

JASON AND SARA: Sure.

MOTHER: What if we could look back and see Zerah, one of the daughters-in-law? Do you think it could go something like this? Shem comes home all excited about a big family meeting and he finds Zerah, his wife, writing in her diary.

Scene 2

(Zerah sitting and writing in her journal. Shem enters.)

SHEM: Writing in your journal again?

ZERAH *(looks up)*: Sometimes I wonder why I do it. Most of the days are pretty much the same.

SHEM: Maybe you'll have something different to put in it soon.

Father's called a big family meeting. He says it's really important.

ZERAH: The last meeting he called was only about buying more land and what crops to plant. I won't get too excited yet.

SHEM: I almost forgot to tell you. The family is coming over here for dessert in a few minutes. It's our time to host.

ZERAH *(all flustered, jumps up)*: Why didn't you give me more warning?

SHEM: Don't worry. Everything looks fine. Mother said she would bring something to eat. *(Zerah fusses around, straightening pillows and other things. Picks up a special vase, rubs it and sets it back down.)*

NOAH: Anyone home?

SHEM: Come in, come in.

(Noah and the rest of the family enter. They all sit down with Noah in front of them. Some sit on the floor. Noah's wife carries in dessert.)

NOAH: I know this is very short notice, but this can't wait. God spoke to me today and I'm trying to sort out all the things He said. It boils down to the fact God is fed up with the way the world is now, and He's going to destroy the earth as we know it.

(All react in disbelief, talk among themselves.)

HANNAH *(sobs)*: I knew it was something dreadful. *(Sobs, Japheth hands her a hankie.)*

HAM: I don't think things are that bad. You must have been dreaming, Father.

JAPHETH: What did He tell you? What about us?

SHEM: God is warning us. We will die. How long do we have?

HAM *(feels whole conversation is ridiculous)*: Just how is God going to destroy the earth?

NOAH: He's sending a flood.

HANNAH: What's a flood? *(Sobs more.)*

JAPHETH: How can He do that?

NOAH: I'm not sure. He said that flood water will cover everything.

JAPHETH: You mean, even if we go on the hill that will also be covered?

SARAH: That would take a lot of water.

HANNAH: I'm scared of water. *(Sobs. Japheth hands her another hankie, pats her hand.)*

HAM: It'll take more water than we have around here.

SHEM: Since God told you what He's going to do, are we suppose to do something?

NOAH: God said we're to build an ark. I'm to take my wife, sons, and their wives into the ark with me. We'll have on board two of every animal. Everything else will perish.

HANNAH: I'm afraid of animals. *(Sobs more, Japheth hands her another hankie.)*

SHEM: Everything? All the people, animals, everything?

NOAH: That's what God said. Everything.

(Everyone is quiet except for Hannah's sobs.)

NOAH: God found only our family worthy to be saved.

SHEM: We can praise and thank Him for that. It won't be easy knowing what is going to happen to everyone else.

JAPHETH: He said we are to build an ark! What do we know about building an ark?

NOAH: I have God's blueprints.

HAM: How are we to keep the ark from leaking?

NOAH: We're suppose to coat it with pitch inside and out.

JAPHETH: What about food? How are we to survive if the whole earth is covered.

NOAH: We're to bring lots of food on board for us and the animals. I believe God will provide what we need.

SARAH: Did God say how long we'd be on the ark? How do we know how much we'll need? I've got some preserves. . . . *(Her voice trails off as she thinks of other things.)*

ZERAH: What about all the animals?

NOAH: Wait, wait a minute. Let me take one question at a time. Let's go back to the ark. It'll be made of cypress trees. About the flood, God knows where He can find enough water to flood the earth to destroy life. It will cover everything for as long as it takes. Zerah, I know how much you enjoy God's creatures. We're to bring two of every kind of animal into the ark, seven of each of the clean animals for sacrifice. When it's time, God will bring the animals to us.

SARAH: How can we take care of all the animals?

NOAH: We don't have to understand all the details yet. The first thing we need to do is get started building the ark.

HAM: What do we know about making an ark? I think it's a crazy idea.

HANNAH: I don't want to live on an ark. *(Sobs, Japheth hands her a hankie.)*

NOAH: Hannah, you'll see the ark won't be a bad place to live. Remember, Ham, I said I have the dimensions from God. It'll have a flat bottom and there will be three decks. We'll have one deck for the animals, one deck for food, and the third deck will be our living quarters. We'll put some of the birds with us so we can hear their cheery songs.

SHEM: You said before it was to be made of cypress trees. I know where there's a good stand of them.

JAPHETH: What will everyone think when we start working on this? Do we tell them what we are doing? Won't they want to come with us?

ZERAH: How will we know when it's time?

NOAH: Wait, wait. Back up a little. We'll have to tell people what we're doing since we may need help with the big timbers. They may think we're a little strange, but they won't care what we're doing until it starts to rain. God will work out the details. He won't send the animals until we have everything ready.

JAPHETH: I can't imagine water covering everything.

NOAH: We can't understand how big God is either. It's something we have to take on faith.

NOAH'S WIFE: I wonder what it'll be like after the flood. Just the eight of us. *(Looks around.)* Why don't we have some of this dessert while we talk. *(Gets up to serve it.)*

SHEM *(quietly to Zerah)*: You really have something to put in your journal now.

(Zerah nods, lights fade as the family is busy talking.)

Scene 3

(Zerah is curled up in a chair writing in her journal. Packing boxes are all around her. She speaks as she writes.)

ZERAH: Abihai was over today. I used to think she was my friend. It seems like the closer the ark is to completion, the more hostile she gets. I tried to explain to her what God was going to do. All she does is laugh at me like the rest of the people. I bet if she truly loved God, He would make room on the ark for her.

It's worse for Shem, the men are even crueler. I hate to take his lunch to him every day and hear the men curse and jeer. They are always joking, "Where's the rain, Noah?" "Did I feel a drop?" "This barge thing will never float," or "How you going to get this thing to water?"

I hate to admit it, but I have doubts. Noah hasn't heard God speak to him since the first time. What if Noah had a dream and it really isn't going to happen? I know God is a holy God and the people are wicked, but to destroy all the people and this beautiful world He made, I don't understand. I guess I'd be more confident we're doing the right thing if God would talk to Noah again. It's been over a hundred years. I wonder how much longer. *(Shakes head and gets up and starts packing.)* I'm not sure what to take. All we will have is what we take with us. I wonder if Shem will be upset if I take this vase. I probably shouldn't, but we'll need some beauty around us. *(Carefully packs it.)*

Scene 4

(Outside the ark. Noah and Zerah stand by a gangplank checking in the animals. She has a clipboard and feather pen. Noah has a small box.)

ZERAH: That was a good idea to balance the weight of all the big animals. Imagine if the elephants, hippos, and rhinos were all on one side and the cows, horses, rabbits and otters on the other side. *(Laughs.)*

NOAH: It's like the animals knew where to go on the ark.

ZERAH: It certainly was a sight to see all those pairs of animals coming from all directions. They walked with such a steady determination. Look at all the birds perched on top of the ark until we're ready to put them in. *(Looks at clipboard.)* According to my list every animal is on board.

NOAH *(looks down)*: We have a few insects coming yet, I believe. Here they are.

ZERAH *(looks down)*: We don't need them. Ugh, leave the spiders out.

NOAH: Now, Zerah, have you seen any lace more delicate and beautiful than a spider's web?

ZERAH: Well, no. Are you really sure God meant for the insects and mice to come along?

NOAH: We have to trust God. He brought them to us.

ZERAH: Can't we keep them in a box or something?

NOAH: Probably a good idea. We wouldn't want to accidentally tromp on them. *(Scoops them up.)*

Scene 5

(Seven of them, all but Shem, are gathered around the kitchen table in the ark. Sound of a big door closing is heard.)

NOAH: What was that noise?

SHEM *(from offstage)*: God shut the door, Father. *(Shem enters.)*

(All face audience as they pretend to look out a window.)

HANNAH: The people are really laughing at us now. *(Sobs, Japheth hands her a hankie.)*

NOAH: After all these years the time is close. *(Looks very sad.)*

HAM: Don't know why you're so glum. Serves them right. They gave us such a bad time.

NOAH: As wicked as they are, it's hard to see them all punished. If only they had turned back to God!

SHEM: It seemed like the closer we got to being finished, the meaner everyone got.

NOAH'S WIFE: Is it raining yet?

HAM: No. How long do we have to wait?

SARAH: This is kind of scary. Did we get on board too soon?

NOAH: No, the animals came and we have all the provisions.

SHEM: God closed the door. It should start raining soon.

HANNAH: I forgot my best cooking pot. *(Sobs, Japheth automatically hands her a hankie.)*

JAPHETH: The door is shut, there's no getting off now.

SARAH: I have an extra kettle. You may have it.

HAM: Why are we the only family on here? Are you sure God spoke to you?

NOAH: I know it was God. Everything else worked out the way He said. Now's a good time to schedule duties. We don't know how long it will take to clean up and feed all the animals.

ZERAH: I'd like to feed some of the animals, especially the big cats.

NOAH: I think we can arrange that. *(Writes it down.)*

SHEM: We'll move some of the food to the animal deck so it'll make it easier for you to feed them.

HANNAH: I'm afraid of all the animals. *(Sobs, Japheth hands her a hankie.)*

SARAH: I'll help you feed some of them, Zerah.

NOAH: Good. Now. . . .

JAPHETH: What's that?

NOAH: It must be the rain.

(All run to look out. They all face audience pretending they are looking out a window. Point out.)

Noah's Wife: The drops are so large.

SHEM: It's coming down hard.

HAM: I can't even see a few feet away.

(Hannah sobs harder, Japheth hands her several hankies.)

ZERAH: Some of the people are leaving.

JAPHETH: They're trying to climb on board.

NOAH'S WIFE: No one's laughing.

NOAH: Let's pray.

Scene 6

(Scene returns to Sara, Jason, and their mother on the couch.)

SARA: You can't end there, Mother.

MOTHER: It's getting late. We could finish it tomorrow night.

JASON: No, Mother, please go on. What happened next?

MOTHER: I guess we'd find Zerah writing in her diary again.

Scene 7

(Zerah is in the kitchen, writing in her journal. Her special

vase is in a box beside her. She picks it up and puts it on the table.)

ZERAH: I'm glad Shem was so understanding when he found this vase in the box the other day. He told me I might as well keep it out so we could all enjoy looking at it. I'll leave it out all the time when the water is calmer. *(Starts to write.)* The water is still pretty rough some days and we bob about like a cork. Sometimes things on the table slide from one side to the other and it's a challenge to eat. *(Smiles.)* It was funny the other night when Hannah was so busy crying that the soup slid right into her lap. With all her tears in it, it wasn't very hot.

It's still raining and water seems to gush up from the earth itself. Each day is pretty much the same as the day before. We've established a regular routine for caring for all the animals. There's nothing to see but water and gray sky. Noah is so calm about everything and Mother Noah is just as relaxed. Shem keeps reminding me I need to go by faith. It worked when we were building the ark and were ridiculed. *(Pause.)* I know God kept His word and it rained, but I'm scared. We go through so much food a day I wonder if we'll run out and starve. *(Pause.)* Maybe if God talked to me, I'd feel better.

It's been a difficult time for all of us living in such close quarters, and that Hannah and her infernal crying. It's her turn to fix dinner tonight, but Ham says she's sick. Sure she is. *(Looks up.)* It's time to start dinner. *(Throws down book and starts slamming cupboard doors or banging pots and pans. Shem enters.)*

ZERAH: This ark isn't big enough!

SHEM: Why do you say that? After I've scrubbed it down from one end to the other, it seems big enough to me. *(Sighs and sits down.)*

ZERAH: It seems like every time I turn around there is Hannah crying. There's enough water outside without all her tears inside.

SHEM: She does cry a lot, but she is the youngest in the family. Is there something else bugging you?

ZERAH: Speaking of bugs, did you check to see that all the spiders are where they're suppose to be?

SHEM: They're all accounted for. What else?

ZERAH: Then there's Sarah. When it's her turn to fix the meals there's no set time. Instead of breakfast we have brunch and dinner. That way she gets out of fixing three meals a day and doing all the dishes.

SHEM: I know. It kind of bothers me too, but she's not a good cook like you are. Maybe what we do bothers her. It's hard to put four separate families together for this long and not have some friction. I find it hard working with Ham sometimes.

ZERAH: I didn't know that.

SHEM: I shovel faster when I get upset, instead of slamming cupboard doors or banging pots and pans. *(He teases and walks over to her and puts his arms around her.)*

ZERAH: God must hate my rotten attitude. I wonder why He chose to save us when we're all sinners. Do you think my fixing meals at the exact time every day bothers Sarah? Guess I should concentrate on her good points. We do have a good time feeding the animals together, particularly the lion cubs.

SHEM: It's a good thing God recognizes our human frailties. I've tried to envision the world as God did with Adam and Eve in the garden. He only asked one thing.

ZERAH *(continues his thought)*: Eve blew it. Now it's up to the eight of us to make a better world. Do you really think we can?

SHEM: Time will tell.

Scene 8

(Zerah is in the kitchen writing in her diary.)

ZERAH: It's been a while since the water started receding. We were all thrown around when we landed on a mountain peak. I'm glad I repacked my vase or it might have gotten broken. The cupboards are a little harder to work because of the angle of the ark, but hopefully we won't be on here much longer. It's so pretty to look out and see the mountains. The sun is shining again, and since the weather has been gray and rainy for so long, it's so bright it hurts my eyes.

Noah sent out a raven one day. It kept flying back and

forth, but it didn't come back into the ark, so we know it found food. Then he sent out a dove and it came right back. After seven days Noah sent it out again, and it came back with an olive leaf. Today he's going to try again.

(Hannah and Sarah enter.)
SARAH: What are you doing, Zerah?
HANNAH: What she always does, writes in her journal. *(Sniffs.)*
ZERAH *(lays aside her journal)*: Right as usual, Hannah. Some day it will be fun to go back and read all I've written.
NOAH *(has a dove on his arm, bustles in followed by his wife)*: Good morning, good morning. It's starting to look promising out there.
NOAH'S WIFE: It's good to see dry land again. The sun feels nice, too.
NOAH *(talks to the dove)*: Well, my little friend, I'm going to send you out today. The last time you brought back a leaf. If you don't come back, we'll know we can leave the ark very soon. *(Goes left stage and his arm with the dove goes behind curtains. All crowd around the window.)*
HANNAH *(crying)*: What are we going to do if it doesn't come back?
ZERAH: We can get off the ark onto dry land and build houses.
SARAH: It'll be good to walk on grass, feel mud, and plant a garden so we can have fresh food.
NOAH'S WIFE: I wonder if the dove will come back.

Scene 9

(Scene goes back to mother and children.)

MOTHER: Noah removed the covering from the ark and the surface of the ground was dry. God told Noah to come out of the ark. It must have seemed strange to walk on the ground again. The first thing Noah did was look around for the right stones to build an altar to give thanks to God. Then he sacrificed some of the clean animals and birds.
JASON: That's when God made the rainbow, isn't it?
MOTHER: God smelled the sacrifice and He said never again

would He send a flood to destroy the earth. The rainbow in the clouds is the sign.

SARA: What about Zerah?

MOTHER: I imagine she and Noah checked to see all the animals got off. I can see her going up and giving her favorite big cat one last big hug because from that time on God put the fear and dread of man into each creature.

JASON: You know that vase she liked so well? I wonder what she did with it?

SARA: I think she looked to see if there were any flowers to put in it.

MOTHER: I'd picture her running back into the ark, getting the vase, and placing it on the altar as her gift to God. *(Pause, looks at watch.)* Guess what? It's time for bed.

SARA: Will you tell us another "could it be" story tomorrow night?

MOTHER: We'll have to think of another Bible character and see what happens.

16

Name That Law

Exodus 20:1-17

This skit takes place during the time of the wilderness wandering of the Israelites. A man and his wife are relaxing after dinner. They are reading the paper and watching TV. The commercials may have included ads for used camels, pull behinds (trailers) or an automatic manna slicer.

The skit involves nine men and four women. It's entertaining but a thought provoking way to present the ten commandments and their meanings.

Characters
MARTA—Wife and homemaker.
EZER—Husband and head of the house.
JOHAB—Newscaster.
JACOB WORTHMORE—Has a used camel lot, a sponsor.
MOSES—Is interviewed on show.
ZILLAH—Lady newscaster and weather forecaster, has a spot on show with household tips.
MASSA—Male commentator.
OBED—Male TV quiz show host.
LAISH—Male contestant.
HELAH—Female contestant.
JODA—Male contestant.
LADY ANNOUNCER—Sells machines, Zillah could be used here.
SALESMAN—Sells tents, could use Massa here.

Props
Cast wears Bible-times clothes.

A simple home is the setting. It should include a table with two chairs, scrolls, cardboard sign. There is a large, lighted TV set made from a rough wood frame large enough for four people to stand behind for the TV show.

Scene 1

(Marta and Ezer are sitting at table reading scrolls. Ezer's has SPORTS written on it, Marta's has WOMEN written on it so the audience can see it.)

MARTA: That looks good.

EZER *(doesn't look up from scroll)*: What's that?

MARTA: Here's a recipe for stir-fried manna.

EZER *(puts down scroll)*: Sounds interesting. *(He gets up and pretends to look out tent flap.)* Must be about time for the evening news. *(Looks up at sky.)* I don't want to miss it tonight. Johab is interviewing Moses. *(Flips on TV and walks back to chair.)*

(Light comes on TV and Johab speaks, but you can't hear him because the sound is turned down. He also jiggles up and down to indicate horizontal hold is malfunctioning.)

MARTA: The set's acting up again, and you might turn the sound up a little.

EZER *(goes back to set, reaches through and touches shoulders of bouncing up and down newscaster, Johab)*: There. That fixed it.

(Moses enters TV.)

JOHAB: Moses, you've had quite an interesting experience recently and we are looking forward to hearing all about your trip up Mt. Sinai. But first a word from our sponsor.

JACOB WORTHMORE *(changes place with Moses and Johab)*: Hi, I'm Jacob Worthmore here with my pet lamb, Fluffy. We're at my used camel lot, and tonight I'm offering a four- foot drive model you can't resist. No money down, small monthly payments, and our ten-day free-exchange privilege. Come down and see us tonight. Bring the kids, we're open every day. *(Exit.)*

(Johab and Moses enter TV.)

JOHAB: Here we are back with Moses. What was it like on the mountain? We were all fearful waiting here at the foot of the mountain, especially when it began to shake.

MOSES: I've talked directly with God before, but it's always an awe-inspiring time. *(Shakes head.)* I really can't describe what it's like to talk to God as a friend. But I never forget He is the Creator of the universe. My desire is to do what pleases Him.

JOHAB: Tell us all about those commandments God gave you.

MOSES: Well, there were ten of them written on stone tablets. God wrote them himself. It took quite a while. When I came back and found the people worshiping a calf, I was furious; and I smashed the stone tablets.

JOHAB: Then, as I understand, you had to write the second set yourself.

MOSES: Well, I chiseled the tablets as God dictated the commandments to me.

JOHAB: Now which law do you feel is most important?

EZER: That's a dumb question. They're all important.

MOSES: Well. . . .

JOHAB: Oh, they're telling me it's time for another word from our sponsors.

(Johab and Moses move so Jacob can be on TV.)

JACOB WORTHMORE: Hi there, I'm still Jacob Worthmore with my pet lamb, Fluffy, and we're here to tell you about a good deal on "pull behinds." This is the best thing invented since chariots, and I'm here to tell you about them. You can pack your tent, cooking supplies, and all your household furniture on this and pull it behind your camel or donkey. The price is right, and we will be open until after dark tonight. Come on in and see us.

(Jacob moves so Johab and Moses can come back to be on TV.)

JOHAB: You were about to tell us about the laws, Moses.

MOSES: The first four laws or commandments are directed toward God. They tell us how we are to react or function in our relationship with God. The other six are moral responsibilities. They are very specific about what we should not do. We all should learn God's laws.

JOHAB: I hear you're writing a book about your experiences with Pharaoh. Have you come up with a title yet?

MOSES: Yes, I'm calling it *Exodus.*

JOHAB: That's a good title. What do you see as the main purpose or theme?

MOSES: I don't want people to forget all of God's miracles in getting us out of slavery in Egypt. This will be an accurate account.

JOHAB: Well, we've come to the end of our time. Let's give a big round of thanks to Moses. We will look forward to talking with him again. *(Moses exits.)*

ZILLAH *(enters TV set)*: As you know, Moses suggested we memorize the laws. I have a hard time remembering them so I've come up with this system. I took one letter out of each law and put them together to make a word. *(She holds up cardboard sign. She doesn't have to say the word.)* GINSPMASWC *(She can point to letters as she says the following.)*

MARTA: Looks like Greek to me.

ZILLAH: G is for God. He's the only true God.
I   is for idols, we're not to worship them.
N   is for God's name, and we aren't to misuse it.
S   is for the Sabbath, and we're to keep it holy.
P   is for parents, and we're to honor them.
M   reminds us we're not to murder.
A   says we aren't to commit adultery.
S   reminds us not to steal.
W   reminds us not to bear false witness and
C   says we're not to covet.
This system has helped me and I hope it will help you. Remember GINSPMASWC. *(Holds up sign again. Hands it through "screen" to Ezer, he takes it.)*

JOHAB: Thank you very much, Zillah. An interesting word. Here's Massa with his evening commentary.

MASSA *(enters TV set)*: Many of us have wondered why these commandments are so important. These laws show us we're sinners and also act as guidelines or guards to keep us from sinning against God. If we follow them, we can live life to the fullest because they protect us from our self-destructive bent.

JOHAB: Thank you, Massa, and now to the weather. What can we expect for the weekend, Zillah?

ZILLAH: We expect the cloud pillar to remain in place tomorrow and, according to our weather map, we can expect more sunny weather. It will be in the high 90's or low IOO's. Back to you, Johab. What do you have planned for the Sabbath?

JOHAB: Nothing, I feel I keep it holy if I don't do anything. I try to bring the commandments into all phases of life. What about you? What are your plans for the Sabbath?

ZILLAH: I like to prepare myself so I'm in the right frame of mind to worship God. I'll take it easy. God designed us to function best if we only work 6 days a week. He also set an example by resting after the creation of the world. Of course He doesn't get tired. I might visit Shua and take her the bulletin from the service since she can't get out.

JOHAB: Sounds like you have it all planned. This concludes our program. Join us again at 11:00 when we will have the latest news and weather for you. Good night. *(Zillah and Johab exit.)*

EZER: I wish they had spent more time interviewing Moses. I don't think they gave him time to really finish any thoughts.

MARTA: That's the trouble with the host. He doesn't really let the guests talk.

EZER: We'll have to stay up until 11:00 to get the news. What would you like to watch now? *(Picks up TV scroll.)*

MARTA: What's on?

EZER: "Tell the Commandments," "What's the Question?" and "Name That Law."

MARTA: "Name That Law" is usually pretty good.

(Ezer gets up and changes channel.)

OBED *(enters the TV screen)*: Welcome to "Name That Law." We want to introduce our contestants, but first we want to tell you about a very special product.

(Zillah enters.)

MARTA: I'm going to get something to drink.

ZILLAH: No, Marta, tonight we have something special for you.

(Marta stops and looks.)

ZILLAH: First, we have an automatic machine which cuts the manna into festive shapes. But that's not all. To go with it, we have a scroll, *"101 Ways to Serve Manna,"* which includes ideas for a picnic or a romantic candlelight dinner with music outside your tent. There are also 99 other ways. *(Holds up scroll.)* Order yours today. Call this toll free number, 800-555-9393.

OBED: Let's bring out our contestants. *(Three people, with cardboard numbers hung around their neck, enter.)* Contestant number one is Laish. *(Each person says hi or nods as name is called.)* Contestant number two is Helah, and for contestant number three we have Joda. Welcome to our show. You all remember how we play the game. Say "Beep" when you know the answer. Let's get right to "Name That Law." Which law is this, I am the Lord your God?

JODA: Beep.

OBED: The answer is what, Joda?

JODA: Number one.

OBED: Now for extra points. What does it mean? Audience, please don't give any hints.

JODA: God reminds us of what He has done in taking us out of Egypt. He wants me to know He is my personal God.

OBED: Very good. Ten points for Joda. Let's go on to the next law. You shall not make for yourself an idol?

LAISH: Beep.

OBED: Laish, for ten points what law is it?

LAISH: Law number two. We aren't to substitute any physical things like the golden calf or put anything else like work or play before God in importance.

OBED: Correct. Contestant number one, Laish has ten points! Ready for the next law? You shall not misuse the name of the Lord your God?

HELAH: Beep.

OBED: Helah, the answer is number _____?

HELAH: Law three. It doesn't mean just swearing but using God's name wrong. We don't show the proper respect by calling Him *(Shrugs and looks up apprehensively.)* "The Man Upstairs."

OBED: Right. You've answered both questions for ten points. And checking our board we have a three-way tie. Let's see which contestant will forge ahead. Remember the Sabbath, *(Pause, no one responds.)* ten more seconds. Remember the Sabbath. . . . Time's up. That's the fourth law. Remember the Sabbath day by keeping it holy. We'll be right back after a word from one of our sponsors.

MASSA *(commercial)*: Family enlarging? Tent too small? Add another room with our prefab rooms. You may have your choice of colors and textures. Come to our warehouse near the mall, right next to the tribe of Gad. Come see us today. *(Exits.)*

MARTA: Did you see that rambler-style tent? Puah and Asher ordered one of them.

EZER: I think they're a passing fad.

MARTA: I don't like the color they chose. It's a bright yellow.

EZER: Well, it'll be easy to find. Oh, they're starting again.

OBED: Here we are back in our studio. Our next question is a different type. What law had a special promise attached?

EZER: That's easy, number five. Honor your father and mother.

MARTA: They aren't very smart tonight.

HELAH: Beep.

OBED: Yes, Helah

HELAH: Loving parents and respecting them: number five.

OBED: That's right. Twenty more points for Helah. That gives her a twenty point lead.

MARTA: He's trying to trick them by going in order.

EZER: Maybe it will get better as they get into a different category.

OBED: We have a new category. We'll continue with the laws in order. All of the laws start the same. See if you can finish the sentence, and the next person in order, will explain the law. If you don't know the answer, we will move on to the next person. We'll start with contestant number one, Laish. Law number six for five points. You shall not ____?

LAISH: You shall not murder.

OBED: Right. And for ten points give the explanation contestant number two, Helah.

HELAH: This includes not just physically killing, but hitting or hurting someone spiritually or psychologically like having bitterness or hate. Even not taking care of your own body correctly is wrong.

OBED: Very good. Joda, can you tell me law number seven?

JODA: You shall not commit adultery.

OBED: Right. Laish, can you give me the explanation?

LAISH: That's easy. Even if one falls out of love or his marriage partner is physically or mentally disabled, he's not to commit adultery.

EZER: I don't think he went far enough. I don't think one should even joke about carrying on with someone of the opposite sex. It can get out of control real easy. There is no excuse in God's eyes for adultery.

OBED: Law number eight?

HELAH: I can't remember. *(Tries counting on fingers, misses turn.)*

OBED: Joda can you tell us law number eight?

JODA: You shall not steal?

OBED: Right. *(Points to Laish.)*

LAISH *(answers questioningly)*: Taking something that doesn't belong to you?

OBED: That's worth five points. Are there other meanings?

LAISH: I can't think of them now.

OBED: Helah, can you give us another meaning?

HELAH: Everything belongs to God, so we would be stealing from Him?

OBED: Well, I was looking for specifics like borrowing when you know you won't pay it back, cheating on tests or taxes, taking supplies from employers or padding the expense account. Those would have been good answers.

Let's talk about prizes for our first-place winner. We have an all expense paid trip to Jerusalem where you will stay in the utmost comfort. For our second and third place people, we have these earrings. They are shaped like the stone tablets Moses made. There are four commandments on one and six on the other. You or that special woman in your life will love them. Let's look at our board to see who is ahead. Third place is Joda, second place is Laish, and Helah is holding the lead. Now back to the exciting conclusion of our game. We stopped with Helah, Joda can you tell me law number nine?

JODA: You shall not tell lies?

OBED: Close, but not quite right. You have ten seconds. Can you add to that? We need the law.

JODA: You shall not gossip, be dishonest, twist the truth. I'm sorry. *(Looks down.)*

OBED: Not quite the right words yet, Laish?

LAISH: You shall not give false witness or testimony.

OBED: Five points to Laish. Joda gave an explanation but he was supposed to give the law. Sorry I can't give you any points for the explanation. Now for the last law, number ten?

MARTA: Covet.

OBED: Helah for five points the tenth law.

HELAH: You shall not covet.

OBED: Right. You have a chance to add to your score if you can give me the explanation, Joda.

JODA: Wanting what someone else has, like a nicer tent, or a brass cooking pot, not being satisfied with what you have.

OBED: Very good. A real close game. Joda has 30 points, Laish 35 but our winner with a trip to Jerusalem has 45 points. Congratulations Helah. We're running out of time, see you next week on "Name That Law!"

(Helah bounces up and down, others hug her.)

MARTA: I wish Joda had won.

EZER: It doesn't seem right somehow. They give prizes like that for things we should all want to know.

MARTA *(gets up)*: I think that's enough TV for tonight. *(Turns it off.)*

Would you like a cup of hot water before we go to bed? *(Walks by table.)* There's still a little manna left, it won't keep until morning. Do you want it?

EZER: Sounds good. *(Gets up, stretches.)* Where's that word Zillah gave me? *(Finds the piece of cardboard with GINSPMASWC on it.)* We should put it up to help us remember the commandments. G is for God.

Love Gleans a Harvest

Book of Ruth

This skit would work well for four to six characters. The soap opera would begin: yesterday we left Ruth as she was leaving her homeland with her mother-in-law. They have arrived in Bethlehem and Ruth needs to find work. Does she go to an employment agency or follow suggestions from Naomi? Can Ruth find happiness in a different country. Will Naomi ever be happy again? Ruth's love and obedience brings her story to a happy conclusion.

Characters

ANNOUNCER

RUTH—A young widow who left her home to go to the land of her mother-in-law.

NAOMI—A sad widow. Her two sons also died. She is returning to her homeland.

BOAZ—A cousin to Naomi and a landowner.

HARVESTERS—Could use cast in unison for one speech since it is a "radio show."

ZADOK—Foreman for Boaz.

Sound Effects Person—Sound effects of background music, newspaper, and dishes are needed.

Props

This skit is performed as an old-fashioned radio program. There is one microphone in the center. When someone speaks they step up to it. The sound effects person is seated to the left. When the page of script is completed, it is dropped to the floor to prevent paper rattling over the air.

Scene 1

ANNOUNCER: Before we find out what is happening in the lives of Ruth and Naomi, let me tell you about "Original Olive Oil." Only the finest ripe olives are used in "Original Olive Oil." The seeds are removed by being partially squeezed and the olives pressed once with a heavy stone to remove the oil. "Original Olive Oil" uses only the oil from the first pressing since we know oil loses some of its purity with each pressing. This fine oil by "Original Olive Oil" prevents bread and meats from sticking during the cooking process. Remember, buy "Original Olive Oil." It is the oil used to anoint kings. *(Background music begins.)* Now to our program. As you remember, Ruth left her homeland with her mother-in-law, Naomi, saying "Don't ask me to leave you. I want to go with you and live where you live. Your people will be my people and your God my God." Ruth and Naomi arrived in Bethlehem yesterday, and Ruth needs to find work. Will she go to an employment agency or follow suggestions from Naomi? Is she homesick? Is she still getting along with Naomi? Today let's find out what Ruth plans to do since she is far from her homeland and kin folks. This morning at breakfast we find Ruth reading the *Bethlehem Banner. (Background music ends.)*

(Sound Effects: rustle of newspaper.)

RUTH: This is pretty discouraging. There aren't many jobs that I'm qualified for available. I know I could learn, but they all say, "Experience required." How can anyone get experience if no one gives her a chance? *(Sighs.)*

NAOMI: I don't know. It's a hard world. I don't know why things happen the way they do sometimes.

RUTH: Well, after our reception yesterday, it seems like a pretty nice world. We have a place to live and food to eat.

NAOMI: Well, I guess I'll have to agree with you there. Of course, Elimelech and I had a lot of friends here.

RUTH: Everyone was so generous, and we have enough food to last us for a while until I can get work.

NAOMI: I certainly didn't plan for you to support me. *(Sighs.)*

RUTH: Things will work out. Remember how you told me God takes care of His people. I can't get over how the whole town of Bethlehem was so excited to see you back. That must make you feel good.

NAOMI: I know this town. It was just the novelty of something different happening.

RUTH: I've been wondering about something you said. I didn't understand what you meant when you asked the women to call you Mara.

NAOMI *(sighs deeply)*: Naomi means pleasant. Mara means bitter. The Almighty has made my life very bitter. I left home with so much, but the Lord has brought me back empty. The Lord has afflicted me. The Almighty has brought misfortune upon me.

RUTH: I know this has been a very difficult time for you, but I'm glad you did come to Moab with your husband and sons.

NAOMI: Maybe if we had stayed in Bethlehem, my husband and two sons wouldn't have died.

RUTH: Then I'd never have met you or married one of your sons.

NAOMI: So here you are a young widow taking on the burden of an old widow.

RUTH: But I love you, Naomi.

NAOMI: I don't know why.

RUTH: Because you are you. I remember how I was drawn to your family because of the way you treated each other. I was awed to learn of your God.

NAOMI: Those were good days, but now I have nothing to look forward to. *(Sighs.)*

RUTH: We have each other and we have God.

NAOMI: That's true and maybe someday my heart won't seem so heavy. *(Sighs.)* I noticed when we arrived that barley harvest time has begun. In our culture we can glean to get what we need.

RUTH: What do you mean "glean"?

NAOMI: From the days of old we have been taught that when we harvest our crops, we are not to touch the edges of our field. This provides food for the poor and alien.

Ruth *(laughs)*: We certainly fit in those categories.

NAOMI: That is also true of the vineyard. Owners can only go through one time and they are to leave any fallen grapes. Since the barley harvest is just beginning . . .

Ruth *(interrupts)*: I can start tomorrow going into the fields and picking up grain.

NAOMI: Very well, my daughter, maybe things won't be so bad after all. I have you.

(Sound Effects: background music plays briefly before announcer speaks.)

ANNOUNCER: We'll return to Ruth and Naomi after a word from our sponsors. *(Music ends.)* "Original Olive Oil" is used by the best physicians to promote healing, and it also keeps your skin moist and soft. Remember to add a few drops of "Original Olive Oil" to your bath water to cleanse your skin. The oil used to anoint kings can be yours. Now, let's return to Ruth and Naomi. *(Background music begins.)* Ruth went out to glean in the fields behind the harvesters. As it so happened, she found herself working in a field belonging to Boaz, who was from the clan of Elimelech. Boaz has just arrived from Bethlehem and greets his harvesters and talks with his foreman, Zadok. *(Background music ends.)*

BOAZ: The Lord be with you!

HARVESTERS: The Lord bless you.

BOAZ: Zadok, who is that young woman over there?

ZADOK: It's the girl from Moab. She came back with Naomi. She asked me this morning if she could pick up the grain dropped by the reapers. I said she could, and she hasn't stopped working except for a few minutes rest in the shade.

BOAZ: I'm going over to talk to her.

(Sound Effects: Walking through grass, rustling sound.)

BOAZ: Good morning.

RUTH: Good morning, my Lord.

BOAZ: Listen, I want you to stay right here in my fields to glean. Don't even think of going to any other fields. Stay right behind my women workers. I've warned the young men not to bother you. When you get thirsty, go and help yourself to the water under the tree over there.

RUTH: You're so kind to me. Don't you know I am only a foreigner?

BOAZ: Yes, I know you are, but I also know about all the love and kindness you have shown your mother-in-law since the death of your husband. You left your father and mother and your own land to come here and live among strangers. May a full reward be given you of the Lord God of Israel under whose wings you have come to take refuge.

RUTH: Thank you, sir. You're so good to me and I'm not even one of your workers!

ANNOUNCER *(background music)*: At lunch time Boaz invited Ruth to eat with his reapers and gave her more food than she could eat. Boaz told the young men to let her glean among the sheaves without stopping her and to snap off heads of barley and drop them on purpose. Does Boaz have a heart interest in young Ruth? We'll find out after another word from our sponsor. *(End background music.)* "Original Olive Oil" is used by all gourmet bakers in their bread. They know that "Original Olive Oil" is pressed only once to get the best quality of oil and only the finest olives are used. So if you want gourmet bread in your home, use only "Original Olive Oil." Now we return for the concluding words of Ruth and Naomi.

RUTH *(excited)*: I'm home, Naomi.

NAOMI *(discouraged voice)*: I'm in here.

RUTH: Look at all I gleaned today! I have a whole bushel of barley after I beat the grain out.

NAOMI *(becomes very cheerful and excited)*: So much! Where in the world did you glean? Praise the Lord for whoever was so kind to you.

RUTH: I went to the field of Boaz. I was scared when I first went into the field, but he treated me like a friend. He even made me sit down to rest when he thought I was tired.

NAOMI: Praise the Lord for a man like that! God has continued his kindness to us as well as to your dead husband. Boaz is one of our closest relatives.

RUTH: He said I should come back and stay close behind his reapers until the entire field is harvested. Do you know that some of the young men even dropped whole heads of barley on the ground for me? I think Boaz told them to because I saw him talk to them and look at me.

NAOMI: Do as he says. You will be safer there than in any other field. Boaz is a relative and not married. I wonder. . . .

ANNOUNCER: That concludes our time today. Will Ruth return to the fields of Boaz? What is it that Naomi is wondering? Is she going to be a matchmaker? Does Boaz have a special interest in the foreign girl from Moab? We'll find out tomorrow. For now, be sure to put "Original Olive Oil" on your shopping list and buy the oil fit for kings. *(Background music to end skit.)*

Applications Accepted

Based on the New Testament

The setting is an employment agency where some of the disciples, some women and a small boy are to be interviewed. The action takes place in Bible times, but modern items such as clipboards, plastic ware, telephones, are added for humor and interest. The final scene occurs 200 years later. The characters are discussing how Jesus used their talents and abilities.

This skit has fourteen characters: eight men, five women and one boy. It shows how God knows our names and uses even the smallest gift we put in Jesus' hand.

Characters

RECEPTIONIST
JAMES
JOHN
JOHN THE BAPTIST
ANDREW
SIMON PETER
PAUL
MARY MAGDALENE
TIMOTHY
MARK
MARTHA
MARY
DORCAS
BOY

Props

The cast wears Bible-times clothes, but there is a mixture of old and modern props: scrolls, sundial, clipboards, several plastic containers, lunch box, desk chair, coffee pot, Styrofoam cups, flowers on desk, end table, six chairs, phone, backpack, business cards, afgan, and briefcase.

Scene 1

(James and John are seated in chairs. The receptionist is seated at the desk. Flowers and a telephone are on the desk. On a small table is a coffee pot and Styrofoam cups. There are six chairs and a sundial at one side of the room.)

JAMES: Wonder how much longer we're going to have to wait, John? *(Stands and paces.)*

JOHN *(walks over to look at the sundial)*: We've been here a good while already. He should see us pretty soon. James, why don't you go ask the receptionist how much longer it will be.

JAMES *(walks to the desk)*: How much longer is this going to take? John and I have been waiting a long time already.

RECEPTIONIST *(looks at scroll)*: It shouldn't be too much longer.

JAMES: I hope not. *(Goes back and sits down.)*

JOHN THE BAPTIST *(enters, wearing a backpack, and goes to the desk)*: I'm John the Baptist. I believe I have an appointment.

RECEPTIONIST: Yes, be seated. You'll be seen soon.

JAMES *(says to John)*: He's a weird one.

JOHN THE BAPTIST *(sits down, pulls out several plastic containers from his backpack, opens two of them and dips "locust" into the honey. He notices James and John watching.)*: Want some?

JOHN *(draws back a little)*: What is it?

JOHN THE BAPTIST: Dried locust. They are good dipped in honey. *(Holds out containers.)*

JOHN: No thanks.

JOHN THE BAPTIST *(offers to James)*: How about you?

JAMES *(shakes head no)*: You really eat that?

JOHN THE BAPTIST: They're quite tasty.

RECEPTIONIST *(answers phone)*: I'll send him in. *(Hangs up phone.)* You may go in now, John.

JOHN *(stands up)*: It's about time. Come on James.

RECEPTIONIST *(to John)*: I'm sorry, I meant John the Baptist.

JAMES *(stands beside John, complaining voice)*: We were here first.

RECEPTIONIST: I'm sorry, but the Master has need of John the Baptist now.

(John the Baptist puts lids on containers, wipes hands on clothes, stands up, walks over and exits. James and John

plop down, cross arms and legs, glare at receptionist.)

JAMES: How can the Master use him?

RECEPTIONIST: All I know is He asked to see him first.

JOHN: I'm not sure why anyone would consider the likes of him. *(Drums fingers on his arms which are still crossed.)*

RECEPTIONIST: The Master can use many types of people.

SIMON PETER AND ANDREW *(Peter rushes in slightly ahead of Andrew)*: We're here. *(Waves scroll.)*

PETER: I'm Simon Peter and this is my brother Andrew. We want to see this Jesus fellow about this ad. *(Holds the ad out and points to it.)*

RECEPTIONIST: Have a seat and you'll be seen soon.

JAMES: Yeah, probably before us. They don't take people in the order they come.

SIMON PETER *(holds out scroll, says to James and John)*: I'm going to be the best follower anyone has ever seen. Says here, "Come follow me and I'll make you fishers of men." Now that's catching pretty big fish. *(Sits down, rereads ad on scroll.)*

ANDREW *(walks over to sit down)*: Sure is a nice day, isn't it?

JAMES: Too nice to be sitting around here. *(Stands and paces.)* How long have we been here?

JOHN *(stands, walks to other side of stage to sundial)*: A little longer than the last time you asked.

PAUL *(enters with briefcase)*: I'm Paul, a Pharisee, the son of a Pharisee. I need to meet with your leader to see if He has all the proper permits. Here's my business card. *(Hands her a card.)*

RECEPTIONIST: If you'll find a seat, He'll see you soon.

(Paul sits down, opens briefcase and pulls out scrolls to read.)

SIMON PETER: If He's looking for smart men with licenses and per-mits and things like that, He's not going to need the likes of us four fishermen. What do you suppose we're getting into?

ANDREW: I'm sure He can use us.

JAMES: The last one that went in was the weird fellow, John the Baptist. He's dressed real strange.

JOHN: Maybe Jesus won't take him.

ANDREW: What does the rest of the ad say?

SIMON PETER: Inexperienced, willing to learn, will train.

JAMES AND JOHN *(lean forward, answer together)*: That's us.

SIMON PETER *(points to scroll)*: Courageous, that's me.

JOHN: Go on. What else?

SIMON PETER: Individualistic. Sure, that's us.

PAUL *(looks up)*: God can use all kinds of people, but it depends on how they keep God's laws. In my mind the more laws you know the more you can obey the living and true God. What do you know about this Jesus fellow? Have you read His doctrinal statement?

SIMON PETER: Doctrinal statement? Learn more laws? This ad doesn't say anything about going to school.

PAUL: The ad said, "willing to be trained."

JOHN: Well, He'd better use us.

Paul *(with a superior attitude)*: Or else you'll have to go back to whatever it is you are doing now? *(Goes back to reading his scroll.)*

(Simon Peter is ready to jump up and fight.)

ANDREW: Let it go. *(Puts hand on Simon to restrain him.)*

MARY MAGDALENE *(enters boldly)*: I'd like to see the Master. *(Sits down next to Paul. She ignores others, primps, chews gum.)*

ANDREW: Nice to have another pretty lady to brighten the waiting room. Can I get you a cup of coffee?

MARY MAGDALENE: Sure why not?

ANDREW *(gets coffee, hands it to her)*: Here you are.

MARY MAGDALENE: Thanks. You been waiting long?

JOHN: I have. *(Jumps up, looks at sundial.)*

TIMOTHY *(enters)*: Oh, there are so many here already. *(Coughs.)* He probably won't want me.

ANDREW: Come in, come in. We don't bite. *(Goes over to Timothy.)*

TIMOTHY *(looks around room)*: Everybody else is older and more experienced. I guess I might as well leave.

ANDREW: I'm sure He can use you.

TIMOTHY: He'll probably decide I'm too young and sickly. Everybody else does. *(Coughs.)*

ANDREW: Relax, it's okay. Give your name to the lady and wait with us.

TIMOTHY: Thanks. *(Turns to receptionist.)* I'm Ti . . . Timothy *(coughs).* He probably won't want me.

RECEPTIONIST *(writes down name)*: Take a seat. He'll see you soon. *(Answers phone.)* Yes, sir. Simon Peter and Andrew, you can go in.

JAMES AND JOHN *(jumps up, protests)*: We were here first.

RECEPTIONIST: I'm sure he has a reason for calling Simon Peter and Andrew first.

(Simon Peter and Andrew exit. James and John pace back and forth, passing each other.)

JAMES: How come we have to wait?

JOHN: Look at the time! *(Points to sundial.)*

MARY MAGDALENE: What you in such a hurry for? It's yukky outside anyhow.

RECEPTIONIST: If you want, you may start to fill out the application form while you wait? That will save time later. *(Hands them clipboards with scrolls on them.)*

MARY MAGDALENE *(saunters over)*: Thanks. *(Asks Paul.)* You gotta an extra pen?

(Paul absentmindedly hands her a pen without looking. Mary Magdalene starts to fill it out.)

JAMES *(sits down, starts to write)*: These dumb pens never write when you want them to. *(Exchanges pen and sits down.)*

JOHN *(sits down and read aloud as he fills it out)*: Name, John, son of Zebedee. Occupation. Fisherman. *(Pause.)* Do you like to write? Never had time to think about it. I might like to write an article or book if there was something worth writing about. I'll put yes.

PAUL *(walks over to desk)*: I'd like to see a copy of the application. Don't you give one to everybody?

RECEPTIONIST: You may fill one out now if you want or with the Master later. *(Hands him one.)*

PAUL: I'd better check out the fine print. *(Goes back and sits down.)*

RECEPTIONIST: James and John, you may go in.

JOHN: Finally. I'm ready, let's go. *(James and John exit.)*

MARK *(enters, walks to desk)*: I'm Mark. I'd like to see the Master. *(Sits down.)*

PAUL: You're pretty young. I'd guess he'd want people a little older who won't change their mind about what they want to do halfway through the job.

MARK: I may be young, but you wait and see. I'll finish the job. Give me a break.

PAUL: We'll see how long you or this preacher last. *(Goes back to reading scroll.)*

MARY MAGDALENE: You may fill out one of these while you wait. *(Waves her clipboard and scroll at Mark.)*

MARK: Thank you. What kind of job do you think He'll have for you?

MARY MAGDALENE: I don't know. I can do all sorts of things.

(Martha and Mary enter.)

MARY: Martha, are you sure this is the right place?

MARTHA *(looks at scroll)*: The ad said, "Followers report to Suite 101 of Building B," and this is it.

(Mary sits down and starts to read scroll she brought with her.)

MARTHA *(goes to receptionist)*: Martha and Mary to see the Master. *(Walks over to sit down, picks up lint off floor, puts it in waste-basket, gets coffee for sister Mary, asks others and gets them coffee. Sits down, takes out hanky and dusts table.)*

RECEPTIONIST *(answers phone)*: Mary of Magdalene, He'll see you now.

MARY MAGDALENE *(says to Mark in particular)*: See you later. *(Starts out and then returns Paul's pen.)* Thanks.

(Martha seated near Paul, neatens up Paul's stack of scrolls he has scattered around. She gets up, fusses with flowers on desk, flips hanky and blows dust.)

MARY *(looks up from scroll)*: Can't you just sit and wait, Martha?

MARTHA: You know I like to keep my hands busy.

RECEPTIONIST *(answers phone)*: Timothy, you can go in.

TIMOTHY *(coughs)*: Thanks. *(Exits.)*

PAUL: He'll have a hard time keeping up with the others as sickly as he looks.

MARTHA: He needs some good home cooking and looking after to plump him up some. *(Picks up his cup, throws it away.)*

DORCAS *(enters with crocheting or handwork, goes to desk)*: My name is Dorcas. *(She sits down and begins working on hand-work.)*

MARY: What are you making?

DORCAS: A rainbow afghan.

MARTHA: It's sure pretty.

DORCAS: Thank you. I enjoy making them for family and friends.

MARTHA: Want some coffee?

DORCAS: Why yes, that would be nice.

PAUL: If you become a follower, do you think you can drag all that stuff with you?

DORCAS: I don't see why not.

RECEPTIONIST *(answers phone)*: Paul and Mark. He'll see you now.

PAUL *(indignant)*: We go in together? My business is different. We don't have anything in common. *(Gathers scrolls and puts them back in briefcase, drops one.)*

RECEPTIONIST: That is what He said.

MARK: Let me help you, sir. *(Picks up a dropped scroll and hands it to Paul.)*

(Paul closes briefcase. Both Mark and Paul exit.)

MARY *(looks up from her scroll to Dorcas)*: I suppose you sew beautifully too, Dorcas?

DORCAS: Well, I make clothes, robes, whatever is needed.

MARTHA: I've been thinking about us women. We'll need to organize so everyone takes her turn cooking. Then if there is free time people can read, sew or crochet.

BOY *(enters carrying modern lunch box, goes to desk)*: Hello. I'd like to volunteer.

RECEPTIONIST: What's your name?

BOY: He knows me. I want to follow Him.

MARY: Isn't that sweet.

MARTHA: I think he'll have to wait a few years before the Master can use him. *(Smiles.)*

Scene 2

(Time has passed. The set is the same, empty cups scattered around. Each group speaks as they enter on one side of stage and exit on other side.)

(John and John the Baptist enter.)

JOHN: I think the idea of a reunion after 200 years is a great idea.

JOHN THE BAPTIST: It'll be good to see those who were among the first followers of Jesus. Do you remember the day we were applying and I offered those dried locusts to you? I won't forget the look on your face. *(Pause.)* Do you care for some now? *(Laughs, acts like he's reaching in backpack for containers.)*

JOHN: No. *(Laughs.)* I believe I'll wait for the refreshments at the party. I remember how upset and impatient James and I were that day. We waited so long and you were called in first to see Jesus. Now I understand, the Lord's timing is always right. You were to prepare men's hearts for His coming.

JOHN THE BAPTIST: My life was short, but my work was completed. By the way, I've read your writings. They really show people that Jesus is the Son of God.

JOHN: It wasn't until after the crucifixion when the Holy Spirit revealed things to us we really understood that Jesus came to set up a heavenly kingdom. *(Exit.)*

(Mary Magdalene and Dorcas are talking as they enter.)

MARY MAGDALENE: Imagine. I was able to serve the Master. He could use even me.

DORCAS: It's surprising how the Master used all of us. All the things I made and gave to others was my service for the Lord. *(Exits.)*

(Simon Peter, Andrew, James and Paul enter.)

JAMES: The world was forever changed because God walked on earth with man.

SIMON PETER: And God allowed us to be a part of it. God can do anything. He changed me from a bungling fisherman to a preacher, healer and author. *(Shakes head.)* Amazing.

PAUL: God can use any yielded life to bring glory to himself. All we wanted to do was glorify and praise God. *(Exit.)*

(Martha and Mary enter.)

MARY *(in wonder)*: His words are so special to me. He said I had chosen what was best, to sit at His feet.

MARTHA: It's so easy to mistake being busy for being spiritual. *(Starts to pick up a dirty cup.)*

MARY: Martha!

MARTHA: Habits are hard to break. *(Leaves cup, both laugh as they exit.)*

(Receptionist and Boy enter.)

BOY: I told you He knew my name.

RECEPTIONIST: He sure did. He used everyone who went past my desk that wanted to be His follower.

BOY *(turns empty lunch box upside down, shakes it, reaches inside)*: You know what? I still don't know how He did it. He fed 5,000 people with my lunch. *(Shakes head, exit.)*

Joab's Lunch

John 6:1-13

Two boys leave with their lunches to go and hear the famous teacher, Jesus. They overhear the disciples talking about feeding the crowd. We know one boy gave his lunch, but how was he influenced that day? What did the other boy do? What do we have to give to Jesus?

The cast includes two boys around eleven years old, two disciples and a small group of people.

Characters

JOAB—A boy about eleven years old.
DANIEL—A friend of Joab's, around eleven.
ANDREW—A disciple of Jesus.
PHILIP—A disciple of Jesus.
CROWD—About a dozen or so people.

Props

Everyone dresses in Bible-times clothes. Cloth lunch bags, bread, baskets are needed. Use plants and other available props to create an outdoor scene.

Scene 1

(Joab and Daniel talk as they are walking.)

DANIEL: Joab, how much farther is it?
JOAB: Not much. Look, Jesus must be on the hill over there. See the crowd of people? Come on, let's hurry!

(Daniel stops and peers into his sack.)

JOAB: What are you doing?
DANIEL: I'm hungry. I'm going to eat part of my lunch now.
JOAB: Not me. I'm going to wait until we get there. Come on.

DANIEL: Okay, but what's the big hurry? *(Takes a bite of his bread.)* What's so great about listening to grown-ups talk?

JOAB: Jesus is different.

DANIEL: What do you mean?

JOAB: My father saw Jesus heal a man.

DANIEL: Really?

JOAB: Remember the guy who always lay near the Sheep Gate? He'd been sick a really long, long time. When Jesus saw him, He told him to pick up his mat and walk.

DANIEL: Did he?

JOAB: He sure did. He was almost dancing when he left. Hurry, maybe Jesus will heal somebody here.

Scene 2

(A group of people stand center stage with their sides to the audience. Joab and Daniel enter stage right so all they see are the backs of the people.)

DANIEL: This is dumb. Let's go home. I can't see anything.

JOAB: Neither can I.

DANIEL: I don't want to stand here staring at people's backs. My feet are tired. I'm going to finish my lunch. *(Takes more bread out of his lunch sack.)* Want some of my bread?

JOAB: Come on, we can squeeze through here. Follow me. *(Grabs Daniel's arm.)*

DANIEL: Oh no, see what you did. You made me drop my bread.

JOAB: Come on, I'll give you part of mine.
    (Crowd remains on stage.)

JOAB: See, we're almost there.

DANIEL: Is that Jesus? *(Points.)*

JOAB: No, I don't think so. That must be Him over there because everybody is listening to Him.

DANIEL: When's He going to heal somebody?

JOAB: I don't know. *(Boys are in front of crowd.)*

    (Andrew and Philip enter left stage.)

JOAB: Listen, I think those are some of His disciples. Let's get closer. *(They move nearer to Andrew and Philip.)*

PHILIP: Why did Jesus ask me where we could buy bread for all these people? Where did He think we were going to get it.

ANDREW: I don't know, but He sent us out to see what we could find.

PHILIP: Are we suppose to manufacture bread out of thin air?

ANDREW: No, but perhaps some of these people know where we could find some food.

PHILIP: Sure and whom are you going to ask? These children?

JOAB: I couldn't help hearing you. You may have my lunch.

ANDREW: Why, thank you.

PHILIP: What good do you think one little lunch is going to do to feed all these people?

ANDREW: Now Philip, don't be so hasty. Let's talk to him for a minute. Do you boys live close to here?

JOAB: No, not really. We started out early this morning to get here.

ANDREW: What are your names?

JOAB: My name is Joab; this is my friend Daniel.

ANDREW: I'm Andrew and this is Philip. We are disciples of Jesus.

PHILIP: Come on Andrew. We can't waste anymore time finding out the names of all the boys in the crowd.

JOAB: I knew you were disciples. Where's Jesus? My father said that He can heal people. Is He going to perform some miracles today?

PHILIP: We're supposed to be looking for food, though any small town in this area isn't going to have enough food to feed all these people even if we went house to house begging bread.

ANDREW: There must be some reason, Philip, why Jesus sent us looking.

JOAB *(interrupts)*: Please take my lunch, sir. *(Holds out his lunch sack.)*

DANIEL: You said I could have part of your lunch.

JOAB: But Jesus needs it. Here's my lunch. *(Holds it out.)*

ANDREW: I'll tell you what, Joab. You hang onto your lunch and I'll take you to see Jesus.

JOAB: Can Daniel come too?

ANDREW: Of course. *(Boys, Philip and Andrew walk to side of stage.)* And what kind of lunch do you have in there?

JOAB *(peeks in sack)*: Two small fish and four barley loaves. No, there are five barley loaves. *(Hands his lunch to Andrew.)*

ANDREW: That sounds like a good lunch. Let's see what Jesus will do.

PHILIP *(takes sack and looks inside)*: Let me see. Those are tiny fish. What can Jesus do with them?

ANDREW: Let's find out what Jesus can do with a boy and his lunch and all these people. *(Exits with Philip, Joab, and Daniel.)*

(Crowd talks among themselves. Andrew and Philip enter.)

ANDREW *(talks to Philip)*: Jesus said we are to have the people sit down.

(They walk over to crowd and the people all sit down. Joab and Daniel bounce in all excited and sit at the front of the crowd.)

DANIEL: What do you suppose they are going to do with your lunch? I'm hungry. I think you should have kept part of it out for us. I wish I had not dropped that last piece of my bread.

JOAB: Shush. Jesus is doing something with my lunch.

DANIEL: What's He doing?

JOAB: He looked up at the sky. Now He's saying something. I can't hear Him.

DANIEL: Look, He's taking out your bread and fish and breaking them up.

JOAB: He's giving pieces of it to Andrew, Philip and some others. They must be disciples, too.

(Andrew comes over to the boys and hands them a basket with food in it.)

DANIEL: Look at all that bread and fish!

JOAB: Where did it all come from?

ANDREW: From your lunch, Joab. Because of your generosity, Jesus took your lunch, thanked God for it, and began breaking it into pieces and putting it in baskets. Look, the other disciples are still taking baskets of food to the crowd.

JOAB: All from my lunch?

ANDREW: All from your lunch! You wanted to see a miracle didn't you? Your lunch is feeding over five thousand people. *(Moves off.)*

JOAB: I can't wait to tell my mother. My lunch is feeding all these people. I can't believe it.

DANIEL: I wish I had waited.

JOAB: Waited for what?

DANIEL: I wish I hadn't eaten my lunch so I could have given it to Jesus.

JOAB: I can't believe what Jesus did with the little bit I gave Him.

ANDREW *(moves over by the boys again)*: Did you get enough to eat?

DANIEL: I can't eat another bite.

JOAB: What are you doing now?

ANDREW: Jesus doesn't want to waste any food, so we are gathering up any food that is left over.

DANIEL: And there's that much left after everybody ate?

ANDREW: Yes, it's a real miracle from God, isn't it? We can never thank you enough Joab for being willing to share your lunch.

JOAB: I wonder what else I can give Jesus?

1000 Paces

Based on Matthew 5:38-48

Simon the Zealot is called upon to carry a Roman soldier's pack for a mile. Simon starts out by counting the steps he is required to go. Halfway through, while Simon is still counting steps, the Roman soldier falls. What does Simon do? It ends as it began with Simon counting paces. How far are we willing to go for our neighbor? This short skit uses three men as characters.

Characters
SIMON—A Jewish Zealot.
GAIUS—A Roman soldier.
ROMAN SOLDIER

Props
Cast wears Bible-times clothes. A dagger, two packs, water bag, and sword are needed.
This skit involves a lot of "walking." This can be done by walking back and forth across the stage area or through the sanctuary if there is an adequate sound system. The skit should begin on the stage and be back on the stage when the Roman soldier falls.

Scene 1

(Gaius stands in the middle of a deserted street. His heavy pack is lying on the ground in front of him. He looks around for a Jew to carry it. Off to the side is Simon who hopes the Roman soldier won't see him.)
SIMON: That Roman dog would stand there. All he's doing is waiting for some Jew like me to come along and carry his heavy pack. When he looks the other way, I should be able to get around the corner. *(He brings out a small dagger and looks at it.)* All I'd like to do is stick this in that Roman pig.

Somebody has to stand up for the Jewish people under oppression from the Romans. *(Replaces his dagger.)* There he's looking the other way, now is my chance. *(He makes his move.)*

GAIUS *(turns and sees Simon)*: Stop!

(Simon stops and reaches for his dagger but doesn't take it out, and turns toward Gaius.)

GAIUS: Carry my pack! *(Marches off without looking back.)*

SIMON *(bends his knees and tries to get a good grip on the pack to swing it up on his back)*: He must have rocks in it. *(He swings it up, and the pack falls back to the ground.)*

GAIUS: Come on, I don't have all day.

SIMON *(swings the pack up, makes a face as it hits his shoulders)*: Swine, I'd love to stick my blade between his ribs. Now I'll be late for our meeting to plan our next attack. *(He counts with each step.)* I have to go one mile or 1000 paces and not a step more. *(He begins to count.)* One, two, three, four.

GAIUS *(turns around to look at Simon)*: Hurry along now, I don't have all day.

SIMON: My mother said it was breaking the sixth commandment to kill but God commanded the Israelites to kill all the Canaanites in the Old Testament. That wasn't murder so it couldn't be murder to kill Roman soldiers. *(He continues counting.)* Fifteen, sixteen. *(Pause.)* My mother changed after she started listening to Jesus the teacher. Turn the other cheek, love your enemies, she's saying all the time now. She used to hate her sister Abagail, now they're friends. That's different than loving Romans. Go a second mile, she said. Ha! She doesn't have to carry any packs.

(Gaius begins to walk a little crooked.)

SIMON: One hundred fifty, one hundred fifty-one. How can you love your enemies? These Romans control our lives. *(Simon reaches for his dagger. Laughs softly.)* I could love a dead Roman. This one doesn't look too healthy and he sure can't walk in a straight line.

GAIUS *(stops and waits for Simon)*: You there, how much farther is it to the next town? *(Wipes his brow.)*

SIMON *(speaks louder)*: Two miles. *(Softer.)* Three hundred forty-five, three hundred forty-six. This is the longest mile and the heaviest pack. Love your enemies. What happened to an eye for an eye and a tooth for a tooth. Take this dog in front of me. Why would I want to love him? He'd be the first to run me through with his sword if he had a reason. Sometimes they don't even need a reason. Halfway, five hundred paces. *(Catches his breath.)*

(Gaius staggers and falls down. Simon throws down pack and runs to Gaius. He looks around. Nobody is near. Fingers the hilt of his dagger and he kneels beside Gaius.)

SIMON: His eyes are closed. It must be the sun but I thought I saw fear and almost pleading in his eyes when he opened them briefly. No, it has to be the sun. Now what am I supposed to do? My mile isn't up but he can't command me to go any farther. Should I take the pack and report in for him? If I show up without the soldier, they'll think I killed him and not wait for me to explain. If this soldier doesn't die, then he can have me hunted down for not finishing the mile. What to do? If the Roman's dead, I'll be blamed anyhow. Love your enemies! Was he really pleading with me or was it my imagination. I didn't think Romans had any feelings. Maybe this one's different.

(He draws out his dagger and runs his hand down the sharp blade and stares at Gaius. He clenches his fist around the handle and takes a deep breath and cuts the thong holding the water skin. He props up Gaius's head and pours water into his mouth.)

GAIUS *(weakly)*: Thank you. I'll be all right in a minute. Let me rest. What's your name?

SIMON: Simon. *(He tries to shade Gaius.)*

GAIUS: I'm Gaius. Is it always this hot here?

SIMON: Sometimes it gets worse. *(Looks up into the sky.)* The sun is a real fireball today.

GAIUS: I'll be all right in a minute. I think I've had too much sun. I'm used to the cooling coastal breezes. Then when I arrived here, I found out my brother had died.

SIMON: That must have been a shock.

GAIUS: I heard Jewish Zealots killed him one night. He was enticed into a dark alley and ambushed.

SIMON *(stands up and walks a few steps away behind Gaius)*: I never thought about Romans having families or feelings. Could it have been this man's brother we killed the other night and then celebrated?

GAIUS: Simon, are you still here?

SIMON: I'm here. *(Goes back and kneels by Gaius.)*

GAIUS: I'd sure like to be home with what's left of my family instead of out here on guard duty.

SIMON: I thought all you Romans wanted to be here.

GAIUS: No, a lot of us would like to be with our families.

ROMAN SOLDIER *(enters with drawn sword)*: Hey you, what are you doing? Get away from him!

SIMON *(jumps up and grabs for his dagger on the ground)*: I'm done for. This Roman isn't going to give me a chance to explain. I knew I should have left him.

GAIUS: Wait, I'm resting. This man was helping me. *(Tries to sit up.)*

(Simon puts his dagger away and helps Gaius into a reclining position. He doesn't take his eyes off the Roman soldier.)

GAIUS: Put your sword away. This man means no harm.

(Roman Soldier puts his sword away with a wild flourish.)

SIMON *(stands up and says softly)*: Am I supposed to be impressed or scared?

ROMAN SOLDIER: What did you say?

SIMON: I said, I've been impressed into service.

ROMAN SOLDIER: We've got to get him to camp. You carry his pack and mine. *(Helps Gaius up. They walk off slowly.)*

SIMON: Just when I thought some of these Romans might be human, along he comes. *(Gestures towards the Roman.)* How am I suppose to carry both packs? Do they think I'm a pack mule? Isn't there a law against having to carry two at a time? If I have to carry two, then I should only have to go half a mile. *(He swings Gaius's pack on his back and the other one he drags.)* Love and pray for your enemies. When did you see your last Roman soldier, Mother? All she'd say is I can decide if I want to love my enemies. Love them, that'll be the day! *(Pause.)* It did work for her. She sure hated her sister. *(Pause.)* I wonder if you understand the enemy if you can make them friends. Interesting thought. *(Shakes head.)* No, it'd never work. No, it can't be done. Well, maybe I'll just look up this Jesus teacher and see how much love He has for these Romans and ask him why anyone should love them. Five hundred thirty-one, five hundred thirty-two, five hundred thirty-three.

The Other Son

Luke 15:11-32

This short skit uses four characters. The prodigal son asks his father's forgiveness for squandering his inheritance. The father is delighted to have his son back home and throws a party, but what do we know about the other son and his life? Let's explore what the older brother may have been like and whether he got over his rebellious attitude.

Characters
RUFUS—The other son, angry and bitter.
HERMAS—A slave who goads Rufus into even more rage.
JULIA—Wife to Rufus who tries to soothe her husband.
FATHER—A loving, forgiving man.

Props
Cast wears Bible-times clothes. Hoe, Jewish music, and sounds of a party are needed.

Scene 1

(Rufus enters, singing or whistling. He has a hoe over his shoulder. As he gets closer to the house, he hears music and meets Hermas.)
RUFUS: Hermas, what's going on?
HERMAS: Master sent me to find you, Rufus. You'll never guess what happened.
RUFUS: It must be something important. I can't remember the last time I saw anything upset you like this. *(Laughs.)*
HERMAS: You won't be laughing long. Your brother is back.
RUFUS *(grabs Hermas's shoulder)*: My brother is back? Did you see him?
HERMAS: Not yet, but I heard your father was really excited.
RUFUS *(he lets go of Hermas's shoulder, his smile is gone)*: Why did he have to come back?

48

HERMAS: Probably ran out of money.

RUFUS: I suppose Father is happy. He spends hours watching for him every day.

HERMAS: Happy isn't the word. I haven't seen your father so exuberant in years. I heard when he saw your brother coming, he ran to meet him. That's not all. He immediately sent for a ring, a long robe, and sandals for him.

RUFUS: Isn't it enough that he took his share of the inheritance? Now he's back to get more. *(Paces back and forth.)*

HERMAS: So whom do you think the music and dancing is for? He even killed a fattened calf.

RUFUS *(flings the hoe down)*: My father killed a calf for a feast for my brother! That's not fair! He never had a feast in my honor. That no good brother of mine always got what he wanted.

HERMAS: Your father is very glad to see him home again.

RUFUS: All these years I've worked hard for my father and never once have I asked for anything extra. What right does my brother have to do this? *(Fists clenched, he strides back and forth.)*

HERMAS: I'd better be on my way. I was told to get more wine. *(Exits.)*

RUFUS *(paces back and forth)*: That no good brother. He always was Father's favorite.

JULIA *(enters, calls softly)*: Rufus, Rufus, are you out here?

RUFUS *(sullenly)*: over here.

JULIA *(walks over to Rufus)*: I've been waiting for you to come home.

RUFUS *(sarcastically)*: Are you having a good time at the feast?

JULIA: So you heard that your brother came home.

RUFUS: I found out when I asked the slave, Hermas, what was going on.

JULIA: Your father is so happy.

RUFUS: Hermas said Father couldn't do enough for him. A ring, long robe, sandals and a feast.

JULIA: He's been gone a long time.

RUFUS: If Father sent you to find me, tell him you don't know where I am. You can go back to the party. I'm not coming in.

JULIA: No one sent me. I thought since it was getting dark you'd be coming in from the fields. Aren't you excited about your brother coming home?

RUFUS: Why should I be? He gets all his inheritance, spends it all, and then comes home to live off my inheritance.

JULIA: Your brother realizes he was wrong. I think you will find he has changed.

RUFUS: He always had a way of sweet-talking people to his way of thinking. All this time I have been working like a slave for my father. Now my brother comes home and everybody falls all over him, particularly my father.

JULIA: But your father loves his children. It's been so painful for him to have his son reject him and all he stands for. It will hurt him to know you won't forgive your brother.

RUFUS: That's too bad. Do you think Father would have done the same for me if I had run off? No way.

JULIA: I'm sure he would, but he's had the pleasure of your company all this time.

RUFUS (mocks): The pleasure of my company. I don't remember him acting like he cared.

JULIA: But do you know something more important? You've had the honor and pleasure of his company. Now admit you enjoyed that special time.

RUFUS: I've had the honor and pleasure of his company anytime I did exactly as he wanted when he wanted it. Sure I did.

JULIA: Your brother didn't have any of that fellowship while he was gone. Those years can never be recaptured.

RUFUS: My brother also missed all the times Father has been angry and out of sorts.

JULIA: Everyone has bad days sometimes. There are times when we have trouble understanding each other too.

RUFUS: You're always sticking up for the other person. Go on in to the party and leave me alone.

JULIA (goes over to him and touches his shoulder): I don't like to see you this way, Rufus.

RUFUS (shrugs off her hand and moves away): Fine, then just go in and leave me alone.

(Julia reaches out to him, turns, and slowly walks away.)

RUFUS (turns and reaches out to her): Julia, wait.

(Julia doesn't hear him and exits.)

RUFUS (turns back and kicks at a clod): It's not fair, God. It's not fair. All his life my brother has been able to do as he pleases. Then he takes his money and spends it having a good time partying. When he's broke, he comes home and Father not only forgives him but welcomes him back. (Pause. Voice gets louder *as anger increases.)* I wonder what ring Father gave him. My guess is he gave him the signet ring and all authority that goes with it. That's mine. I'm the oldest. I stayed home, did all my father asked me to do, and didn't complain. But did he ever give me a feast? No, he never even killed a goat, let alone an expensive fattened calf. *(Yells.)* It's not fair, God!

FATHER *(enters)*: Rufus, Rufus, is that you? I've been looking all over for you. Did you hear your brother is home safe and sound?

RUFUS: How could I help but hear?

FATHER: Come in and join us. We're having a great time welcoming your brother home again.

RUFUS: I don't feel like it.

FATHER: Nonsense. Come in. He's been asking where you are.

RUFUS: No, Father, I don't want to come to the feast. In case you haven't noticed, I've been working in your fields all day and I'm tired.

FATHER: Of course, I know you have been working—all the more reason to relax and forgot all your effort.

RUFUS: I'm not interested.

FATHER: It grieves me to listen to all the things your brother has been through.

RUFUS: It's his own fault.

FATHER: Can you believe he was going to ask me if he could be my hired hand?

RUFUS: You should have hired him. He spent all of his inheritance, now he comes back and you treat him like a king.

FATHER *(doesn't seem to hear what Rufus said)*: It seems the pigs he fed ate better than he did, so he decided to come home.

RUFUS: Where else could he go? He knew he could always come back here.

FATHER: That's true enough. *(Sadly and then brightens up.)* Have you no compassion? Your brother knows what he did was wrong, and he is the first to admit it. He's really sorry and now he's home. He was lost and now is found.

RUFUS: Hooray!

FATHER: There haven't been a lot of things I've really asked you to do for me. But Son, all our family and friends are in at the feast having a good time. I'm asking you to join us.

RUFUS: No.

FATHER: Please, Rufus, I'm pleading with you. Make an old man's heart happy that I may enjoy both of my sons.

RUFUS: Look! All these years I've been slaving for you and never disobeyed your orders. Yet you never gave me even a young goat so I could celebrate with my friends. But when this son of yours who has squandered your property with wild living comes home, you kill the fattened calf for him! *(Turns back on father.)*

FATHER: My son, you are always with me, and everything I have is yours. Haven't you enjoyed the riches of my table three times a day?

RUFUS *(wheels around to face Father)*: Yes, Father, but who did all the work to put it there? Me. That's who!

FATHER: Haven't I clothed you and given you and your family a nice place to live?

RUFUS: But who did all the work? Now your son comes home. You give him a long robe. I'm the older brother. I should be the one with the long robe of distinction. I should have the signet ring of authority.

FATHER: But Rufus, he is my son, just as you are. Haven't you enjoyed time with me as we got to know each other's heart, my son?

RUFUS: I thought I knew and understood you. But how can you not only forgive him but welcome him back with open arms?

FATHER: He's my son. I want to celebrate and be glad because this brother of yours was dead and is alive again. He was lost and is found. Please come in. *(Reaches out.)*

RUFUS: No, I'm not celebrating with you. *(Stomps off.)*

FATHER *(reaches out to Rufus)*: My son, my son. Your bitterness and hatred will not keep you warm. *(Holds imploring hands to the heavens.)* Dear Father God, I am so happy that my son who was lost is now found, but now my other son is lost in his bitterness and anger. I love him so much and it grieves me to see him turn away from me and You. I understand more completely how You hurt when we turn away from You. I ask for healing in our relationship. *(Bows head in continuing prayer.)*

The Investors

Matthew 25:14-30
Luke 19:12-27

This is a short skit using six characters. The president of a company calls in three of his employees and puts them in charge of his money while he's on a business trip. One man calls his broker and makes wise investments in stocks, bonds, real estate and precious metals. The second man invests in a sheep ranch and a bagel bakery. The third man buries his money in the ground because he's afraid of the responsibility. The three men are accountable for their stewardship as we are accountable to God for what He gives us.

Characters

MATTHEW—Top man in company. He's worked his way up paying attention to small details and has a willing spirit.

SIMEON—A man working his way up the corporate ladder, eager to learn, willing.

JARIUS—A relative newcomer with potential. He feels inferior and wants the glory of a top position without working for it. Rather lazy.

PRESIDENT BENJAMIN—A successful businessman of a large corporation. He's testing his men while he is gone to see how well they handle responsibilities, large or small.

THOMAS—He consults with Matthew about business opportunities.

DAN—He becomes a business partner to Simeon.

Extras for party scene noise.

Props

Everyone wears Bible-times clothes. A table, chairs, briefcases, scrolls and papers, calculator, a red bandana, cowboy hat, mugs, metal box, plant, shovel and two comfortable chairs are needed.

Scene 1

(Simeon and Matthew are waiting in the boardroom. Jarius enters.)

JARIUS: Anybody know why the big man called this meeting?

MATTHEW: Good morning to you too, Jarius.

JARIUS *(nods)*: Morning, Matthew, Simeon.

SIMEON: I don't know why this meeting was called, but we'll find out soon. Our president is never late.

JARIUS *(sarcastically)*: Always the epitome of everything good.

(Benjamin enters.)

MATTHEW *(rises immediately to acknowledge the president)*: Good morning, sir.

SIMEON *(jumps to his feet)*: President Benjamin.

(Jarius stands up halfway.)

BENJAMIN: Please sit down, gentlemen. What I have to discuss won't take very long this morning. You may have heard the rumor going around that I'm going out of town for a while. This rumor happens to be true.

SIMEON: Will you be gone long, sir?

BENJAMIN: I'm not sure. That's why I called this meeting. I need you men to take care of some of my investments while I am gone.

JARIUS: What do you mean?

BENJAMIN: I've promised my wife I would leave all business behind; and with the volatile markets, I need someone to watch my investments. Some of my bonds matured. Since I'm leaving this morning, I don't have time to reinvest. This is what I am asking you to do. Matthew, I've been watching you for a long time. No matter what job I've given you to do, you accept it and do it with a willing heart. Remember when I asked you to clean my barn one weekend?

MATTHEW *(laughs)*: Yes, sir, I remember well.

BENJAMIN: There was nothing wrong with my servant that day, I was testing you to see if you were a big enough man to do a menial job. Now I am asking you to take these five bonds and invest them for me. Each one is worth about two thousand dollars.

MATTHEW: Yes, sir. What stocks or bonds would you like me to invest in?

BENJAMIN: Think of it as another test, Matthew. You have a very logical and methodical mind. You'll chose something good I know. *(Gives him papers.)*

MATTHEW *(takes papers)*: Thank you, sir. What an honor. I will invest this wisely for you.

BENJAMIN: Simeon, you haven't been with the company quite as long but I trust your creative approach to life. I'm giving you the responsibility of two bonds, again each is worth a couple thousand dollars. *(Hands him the papers.)*

SIMEON *(take papers)*: Thank you, Sir. I, too, am honored. An investment idea has already entered my mind. Would you like to hear it?

BENJAMIN: No, Simeon, you can tell me about it when I return. Jarius, you are a relative newcomer to the firm, but I see a lot of potential in your abilities. I'm giving you one bond to invest for me.

JARIUS: What if I invest and I lose your money?

BENJAMIN: You have worked for me long enough to know the type of things I invest in. I trust your judgment.

JARIUS: But if I lost your money, then I would have to pay it back out of my salary right? That would take years and years.

BENJAMIN *(isn't too pleased with Jarius' response, he frowns)*: If I didn't think you had the ability, I wouldn't have asked you to invest for me.

JARIUS: Yes, sir.

BENJAMIN: Now, if there are no further questions, I will take my leave. The camel caravan will be leaving soon and I don't want to miss it. Is that all? *(Looks around quickly.)* Good-bye, gentlemen. *(Exits.)*

MATTHEW *(jumps to his feet)*: Good-bye, sir. I'll take good care of your money. *(Shuffles the papers Benjamin gave him.)* Well, I don't know about you fellows, but I'm going to call my broker and begin to invest this money right away. *(Exits.)*

SIMEON *(stands up)*: I heard about a good investment on a sheep ranch. I think I'll see if that is still available. It would have helped to know how long a term of an investment to make. *(Picks up his bonds, stops at door, and turns to Jarius.)* What are you going to do with yours, Jarius?

JARIUS: I'm not sure. I don't know why President Benjamin stuck us with the responsibility to make more money for him. This talent is worth less than a thousand dollars and most brokers don't want your business unless you have a lot more than that to invest.

SIMEON: Well, I'm sure you'll think of something. Would you like me to help you?

JARIUS *(looks at his bond)*: No, no, he gave it to me to do something with it. He sure didn't trust me with much—one lousy bond.

SIMEON: It isn't so much the amount as what you do with what he has given you. If you prove yourself faithful with a little, he'll give you more. I'd love to have seen Matthew cleaning out that barn. *(Shakes head and laughs, exits.)*

JARIUS: Sure it's easy for them, they have more than one crummy talent to make more money.

Scene 2

(Matthew is sitting at his desk working and Thomas stops by.)

MATTHEW: Good morning, Thomas. Thank-you for coming by so promptly. I would have come over to your brokerage office, but I needed to clear up some odds and ends here.

THOMAS: I don't mind at all. In fact it's a lovely day for a walk. I must admit, Matthew I was intrigued by your message. All of a sudden you have a good share of money to invest. Did you have a rich relative die and leave you some money?

MATTHEW: No, nothing like that. Our president surprised all of us today when he announced he was going on a business trip.

THOMAS: That's not unusual for him as I recall.

MATTHEW: True, but this time he gave three of us in supervision some money to invest for him.

THOMAS: How much money are we talking about?

MATTHEW: He gave me five talents.

THOMAS *(whistles in surprise)*: That is a tidy sum. How much investment time do you have?

MATTHEW: That's the problem, I'm really not sure.

THOMAS: Well, I think I brought just the thing for you. I have some short-term safe investments and longer terms like hospital bonds. We can make up a good portfolio with a nice combination of long-and short-term investments. *(Pulls some papers and a calculator out of his briefcase.)*

MATTHEW: That sounds good to me. What about investing in some utility stock? I'm sure you have some good tips.

(They scoot their chairs closer together as Thomas shows the papers to Matthew.)

THOMAS: Here's what I'd recommend.

Scene 3

(Simeon and Dan are at a restaurant having coffee.)

SIMEON: Thanks for meeting me in town today, Dan.

DAN *(cowboy hat, red bandana around his neck)*: I needed to come in for supplies anyhow. What the big mystery?

SIMEON: Are you still thinking about expanding your sheep ranch?

DAN: I've put that idea on hold for now. I need over one thousand dollars to buy some new breeding stock and to hire another shepherd.

SIMEON: What if I told you that if we can agree on my profit, I have the money for you?

DAN: And the moon is made of green cheese and people are walking on it.

SIMEON: I'm serious, Dan.

DAN *(looks cautiously around)*: Now where did you find that kind of money? Did you embezzle it or rob a bank?

SIMEON *(laughs)*: Nothing like that. Our president went out of town and he gave us some money to invest for him. I thought about your need and I think sheep ranching is a good investment. The temple will always need lambs for sacrifice and the people need them for special meals. Then there's the side industry of hides and all one can do with them. It seems like a good investment.

DAN: You're aware there is a bit of a risk? Even though we have good shepherds, there are some sheep that get sick, wander off, or wild animals kill them.

SIMEON: I'm aware of that. That's why I am going to hold back part of the money to invest in something else like the Bagel Bakery.

DAN: You sure diversify. Well, if you're sure you want to do this. I can get in touch with Joshua. He still didn't have a buyer the other day for his sheep.

SIMEON: Partners then?

DAN *(reaches out to shake hands)*: Partners.

Scene 4

JARIUS *(Looks all around. The whole time he acts very furtive. Carefully he measures off distances. He begins to dig and periodically looks around. He stops digging to reflect.)*: You can sure tell who the boss likes in our office. Eight hundred fifty dollars is all he gave me to invest. If he had given me two or three thousand dollars, I could have done something really important. But no, he doesn't think I'm worth very much. If the bank was robbed or closed because of bad investments how would I ever be able to replace that money? Besides the interest rates are so low it wouldn't make it worthwhile. The stock market goes up and down, and it dropped today. If I'd invested in that, I'd be behind already. No, the safest thing I can do with the talent is bury it. *(When he decides the hole is deep enough, he removes the talent from a hidden pocket, wraps it up and puts it in a metal box. He looks all around. He puts the box in the hole, and covers it up with dirt and a plant.)*

Scene 5

(Matthew and Simeon are in the board room.)

MATTHEW: It will be good to see President Benjamin again. He's been gone a long time. I bet he's anxious for a report on how we did with the talents he gave us.

SIMEON: I'm sure glad he didn't come back a year ago. Things looked pretty dark at that time. I invested in a sheep ranch and we had a run of bad luck. Fortunately my other investment in the Bagel Bakery made up for it. I doubled what President Benjamin gave me.

MATTHEW: Good for you. I, too, was pretty successful. The hospital bonds matured so I have all the interest that paid and the initial investment. I doubled the five bonds he gave me. I think he will be pleased.

SIMEON: I wonder where Jarius is and how he did. I have a feeling that he didn't make much of an effort.

MATTHEW: I asked Jarius right after the President left if he had found something to invest in and he was very evasive. He mumbled something about being afraid to put it in a bank since the day before it had been robbed and the stock market was down.

SIMEON: I got the feeling from the beginning that he felt he was entrusted with so little it wasn't worth worrying about.

MATTHEW *(looks out the window)*: Well, we should be finding out soon both President Benjamin and Jarius are coming now.

SIMEON: That's good. Benjamin wants punctuality and results.

(Jarius enters just before Benjamin and quickly takes his seat. He brushes at his dirty hands.)

BENJAMIN: Good morning, gentlemen. It is good to see each of you again. I trust the years have been good to you and to my money. *(Laughs.)*

MATTHEW: It's good to see you again, sir. Things just aren't the same when you're not around.

BENJAMIN: Well, let's start with you, Matthew. How did you do with the five talents I gave you?

MATTHEW *(opens his briefcase and pulls out a lot of papers)*: I think you will be pleased, sir. I immediately went to the brokerage house and made these investments for you. I am pleased to return your five bonds and five more that I made for you.

BENJAMIN: Well, done. You're a good and faithful servant! I appreciate your being faithful with a few things through the years and now, when I gave you more responsibility, you came through beautifully. To show my appreciation, I'm putting you in charge of my Jerusalem office. To celebrate your promotion, I want you to come to the house for dinner tonight so you can share my happiness!

MATTHEW: Thank-you, sir. I would be honored to come.

BENJAMIN: And Simeon, what report do you have for me?

SIMEON: I really appreciated your trusting me to make investments for you. I invested in a sheep ranch, but because of many variables, I thought it best to hold some back for another venture. The sheep ranch did run into a few problems, but we recouped and my other venture, the Bagel Bakery, did well. Here is your bond money back and the equivalent of two more that I gained.

BENJAMIN: Well done, Simeon. You are a good and faithful servant! You, too, have been faithful with a few things and I will put you in charge of my Bethlehem office. I want you to come to dinner at the house tonight and share my happiness.

SIMEON: Thank you, sir. I would be honored.

BENJAMIN: Well, Jarius this has been a good day. Tell me what exciting venture you tried with the one talent I gave you?

JARIUS: Well, I know you are a hard and shrewd man. You expect a return on your investments where you haven't done any work. I was afraid I would lose your money in some venture, so I hid your talent in the ground. See, here it is: what belongs to you. *(Smoothes out the wrinkles before he holds it out.)*

BENJAMIN *(stands up and angrily paces back and forth)*: You wicked and lazy servant. So you think I'm a hard and shrewd man do you? Well, if that is the case, you should have put my money in the bank and at least I would have received a little bit of interest on my money. Simeon, take the talent from Jarius and give it to Matthew.

(Simeon gets up and walks over and gets the paper from Jarius and gives it to Matthew.)

BENJAMIN: Everyone who has will be given more and will have plenty. Jarius, what you have will be taken from you. *(Points to the door.)* You're fired!

(Jarius exits.)

Scene 6

(At the party. Matthew and Simeon are in comfortable chairs talking. There is a sound of music and people laughing and having a good time.)

MATTHEW: I could get used to this kind of life very easily. *(Looks around appreciatively.)*

SIMEON: This is nice. My wife was so excited when we found out she could come. She's always wanted to see the inside of this place.

MATTHEW: I guess wives are all the same. Rachel was very pleased and immediately announced she had nothing to wear. *(Laughs.)*

SIMEON: It's too bad about Jarius. I tried to talk to him several times about what he was doing with his bond money. He felt he wasn't given enough to be challenged with, so he didn't want to be bothered. I felt he didn't want to take time to really figure out what to do and he didn't want to take a chance and lose the money.

MATTHEW: I guess my grandma taught me well. When I was a child, I wanted a bigger allowance because I thought I knew what to do with it. But usually the day after I got it, it was gone. Then I wondered why my parents wouldn't trust me. My grandma knew what was going on. She said if I managed my small allowance well, it would prove to my folks I could handle larger amounts, and this was true in all areas of life not just financial. That was her favorite lecture.

SIMEON: Grandmas must be pretty smart. Mine always said, "It's what you do with what you've got."

Choosing the Best

Luke 10:38-42

In this skit of five characters we see more of the spiritual side of Martha. Martha feels badly about Jesus' rebuke and Mary comforts her. We see that God made different kinds of people. We all need to grow spiritually and nurture our inner life. Jesus is our example. He came to serve.

Characters
MARTHA—Busy homemaker.
JULIA—Servant girl.
MARY—Reflective, quiet.
SARI—An upset friend, Martha comforts her.
JAMES—A disciple.

Props
Everyone wears Bible-times clothes. Needed are a table, two or three chairs, a pile of scrolls, a writing tool, another table with pottery containers on it, cups and pastries.

(Martha is sitting in a chair by a table in the common room. There is a doorway to the outside. Julia stands at the doorway waiting for Martha to notice her. Finally she clears her throat to get Martha's attention.)

MARTHA *(raises her head)*: Yes, Julia.

JULIA: Excuse me, mistress, but the cook sent me to ask you where she should prepare the meal today. She's willing to cook in the courtyard so the smoke won't fill the house again.

MARTHA *(walks to doorway and looks at sky)*: It's not raining now and the sky looks pretty clear. Tell her to begin outside. That sudden rainstorm couldn't have happened at a worse time yesterday with Jesus and the disciples coming. *(Shakes head.)* What a mess. Jesus and his men were trying to get their clothes dried out and cook transferring everything to the smaller portable stove in here, which meant all the smoke and cooking odors filled the house.

JULIA: It was pretty hectic for a while. I'll go tell the cook. *(Exits.)* *(Martha sits back down, deep in thought. She nervously taps a stylus on the table.)*

MARY *(enters yawning and stretching)*: I could have slept in today but I wanted to help you get everything organized this morning. *(Notices Martha isn't doing anything.)* Martha, you're not doing anything, you're just sitting. What's the matter? *(Hurries over to her)*.

MARTHA: Nothing. *(Wipes eyes.)* I'm fine. I need to check to make sure cook doesn't need anything. I don't know what's wrong with me. *(Starts to get up.)*

MARY *(kneels in front of Martha and holds her hand)*: You're not going to do anything until you tell me what's wrong.

MARTHA: I've really been doing a lot of thinking because of what Jesus said to me last night.

MARY: He always says so much for us to think about.

MARTHA: You know what I mean. When I came storming in to complain about you not helping me, and Jesus said you had chosen the better part.

MARY *(quietly)*: Oh yes. I knew that really upset you.

MARTHA: It really hurt. *(Sobs.)* I wanted everything just right for the Master.

MARY: Of course you did. Jesus knows that.

MARTHA: Everything went wrong besides the rain. The cook put too much garlic in the stew and those pastries didn't turn out right. *(Wipes eyes.)*

MARY: Did you ever see such a bunch of sorry looking men when they all arrived? They sure made a mess on your nice clean floors.

MARTHA: I'm sorry I got so upset with you for not helping me.

MARY: It's all right Martha. If I had helped you a little more before Jesus and His disciples came, you wouldn't have felt so much pressure. I should have helped more when they came. When Jesus is around, I don't want to miss a single word He says.

MARTHA: I didn't need to try new recipes that would take extra preparation time. I could have fixed a simpler dinner.

MARY: But Martha, that's you. You enjoy trying new recipes and setting a fine table. Remember how Jesus complimented you on the dinner and how beautifully it was served?

MARTHA: That's true.

MARY: As I remember, Jesus had second helpings of it.

MARTHA: He did, didn't He. *(Smiles.)*

MARY: It was an exceptionally good dinner. Did you see how much Peter ate? I thought he'd never get full.

MARTHA *(laughs)*: You'd think Peter had a hollow leg the way he ate.

MARY: The rest of the disciples ate their share, too.

MARTHA: But, Mary, Jesus is right. When I neglect my spiritual life and get too busy "doing," I always run into problems. I need to make sure I set aside a time to pray and reflect on what our Lord has said.

MARY: And I need to be sure I don't neglect my duties around here; because if I do, that doesn't honor God either. I'll begin now by seeing how cook is doing. *(Exits.)*

(Martha paces back and forth, looks out the door and sits down again.)

SARI *(enters very upset)*: Martha, I know this is an awful time for a social call because you have company, but I have to talk with somebody.

MARTHA: There's always time for you. Sit down. Let me get you something to drink and one of my special pastries from dinner last night. Then you can tell me your problem. *(Martha flits around to get a pastry and something to drink and puts it on the table and sits down.)* How can I help?

SARI: I don't know where to begin. Well, I thought Priscilla was my friend. She got real upset and said some mean things to me. I'm ready to go over and tell her what I think.

MARTHA: Perhaps something happened to her you don't know about and she had to lash out at someone. You, unfortunately, were there.

SARI: I don't know about that, but I don't appreciate it, I'll tell you.

MARTHA: Jesus said to love your enemies and bless them that curse you.

SARI: What does a poor, itinerant preacher know about such things?

MARTHA: Jesus is more than that. He heals the sick and performs all kinds of signs and wonders. He knows the problems of the heart and sees beyond outward appearances.

SARI: Well, I've heard He's done some pretty impossible things. *(Takes a bite of pastry and looks at the piece in her hand.)* My this is lovely. I must have the recipe. What do you mean He sees beyond outward appearances?

MARTHA: I won't go into details, but last night I said something without really thinking about it; and He knew what my real problem was.

SARI: Do you think He'd be able to help me?

MARTHA: I'm sure of it. I learned that sometimes it isn't so much what we say but how we say it. Sometimes I blurt out the first thing that pops into my head, and that usually gets me into trouble.

SARI: I think I'd like to meet the man, Jesus. What do you think He would tell me to do about Priscilla?

MARTHA: Jesus would say to love her, to seek the best for her.

SARI: I don't know if I'm ready to love Priscilla right now, but I would like to meet Him.

MARTHA: Jesus and His disciples will be back tonight. Why don't you drop in and meet Him?

SARI: I'd love that. Well, I guess I had better get my shopping done. Thanks again for the goodies and the talk. I'll see you later. *(Sari exits.)*

JAMES *(enters through courtyard door)*: I'm amazed, Martha. Already you have the cook fixing something that starts the taste buds working.

MARTHA: Is the Master up yet?

JAMES: I heard Him get up very early. He's probably gone somewhere to pray. *(Looks outside.)* Looks like we're going to have a nice day.

MARTHA: Let me get you something to eat.

JAMES: I'm in no hurry. I ate too much last night. *(Pause.)* You seem a little sad this morning, Martha. Can I help?

MARTHA: It's nothing. *(Starts fussing around.)*

JAMES: I know you too well, Martha. Let me guess. You're upset because of what Jesus said when you asked Mary to help you, right? I saw the pain in your eyes.

(Martha begins to cry, wipes her eyes.)

JAMES *(goes to her and puts his arms around her)*: Now what would we do if you didn't make a big fuss over all of us?

MARTHA: I wanted everything to be so nice and everything went wrong.

JAMES: I know, we arrived like a pack of wet rats making a mess all over your nice clean house. But you know that was the best stew I've ever tasted.

MARTHA: You're just saying that. *(Wipes eyes and backs away to look at James.)*

JAMES: No, I mean it. When we're away from home, we don't get anything half as good as what you fix.

MARTHA: Jesus didn't seem to care.

JAMES: Not true, Martha, and you know that. It's that He's so aware of all the hungry souls that need to be filled that physical food isn't important.

MARTHA: But I should have been in there learning from Jesus. I try to be spiritual, but I see so many things that need done around the house.

JAMES: God made different kinds of people. If the world was full of Marys sitting around, who would feed and clothe them? The Marys of the world need to be sure they are involved in some service. You have some of Mary in you.

MARTHA: What do you mean?

JAMES: There is a spiritual depth in you, Martha.

MARTHA: You're not saying that to make me feel better?

JAMES: No. I mean it. What the Marthas of the world need to do is make a special effort to grow spiritually and nurture their inner life and not become all wrapped up in being busy and doing all the time. Jesus is our example. He came to serve.

MARTHA: Thank you, James, that makes me feel much better. *(Wipes eyes and smiles.)*

JAMES: Now if that offer of something to eat still holds, I think I'm ready.

MARTHA: Sit down and I'll fix something special for you. *(Starts fussing around.)*

JAMES: There you go again, fussing over someone. *(Laughs.)* I like it.

MARTHA: While I'm fixing something, tell me more about what Jesus said about the price of discipleship.

Front Page Story Squelched

Matthew 27

This skit takes place after the crucifixion of Jesus. It tells the crucifixion story from a different viewpoint. It begins at the newspaper office of the *Jerusalem Journal.* Various reporters are sent out for stories dealing with the crucifixion. Asher, the city editor, has to make a decision for the front page story. Did Asher give in to a payoff and squelch the biggest story of all time? Would we be brave and speak the truth or would we give in to a pay off?

This skit has nine main characters: five men, two women, two boys, and a small group.

Characters
ASHER—Hardened city editor of the *Jerusalem Journal.*
JUDE—Relaxed reporter.
JOSEPH—Hotshot reporter.
JENNIFER—Reporter.
COPYBOY
DARIO—Reporter.
NEWSBOY
MARY MAGDALENE
MARCUS—Friend in the temple.
CROWD SCENE

Props
All characters wear Bible-times clothes. You will also need two or three tables or desks, chairs, broken pottery, coins, and lots of scrolls and writing utensils.

Scene 1

(Asher is under his desk trying to piece together shards of clay. Jennifer and Dario are at desks.)
JUDE *(enters)*: The earthquake is over, you can come out from

under the desk.

ASHER: The earthquake knocked my notes on the floor. I'm trying to piece them together.

JOSEPH *(enters very excited)*: I can see part of your desk. Can't remember the last time that happened.

ASHER *(comes out from under desk)*: Forget the condition of my desk and see what damage has been done. During the last earthquake, a day or so ago, the veil in the temple got ripped apart. What did you see on the way in?

JOSEPH: From what I heard so far, this earthquake was centered by a garden where that Jesus fellow was laid. Seems like strange things are going on. The guards are afraid. Some say the body of that Jewish blasphemer is missing from the tomb. Sounds like I might get a Pulitzer prize story out of this. Where do I start?

ASHER: Never mind about prizes. Let's see what we can find out before the evening edition. There should be a lot of excitement over at the temple. Joseph, get over there and see what they have to say about all this. It'll be fun to see them all scurrying around. This might even be worth an extra edition. Copyboy! Copyboy!

JOSEPH: I'm on my way. *(Picks up stylus and piece of pottery to write on. Exits.)*

JENNIFER: I wonder if the disciples managed to sneak the body away with the guards on duty?

ASHER: I want you to get a woman's angle on this, Jennifer. See if you can get an interview with the mother of this Jesus or one of the ladies who followed Him. See what you can pry out of them.

JENNIFER: Sure boss. That's better than having to do recipes for the women's page. *(Exits.)*

COPYBOY *(enters on the run)*: Yes, sir.

ASHER: You tell the printers to save space on the front of the scroll for some big news.

COPYBOY: Yes, sir. *(Runs out.)*

ASHER: Who else is here? Dario, nose around and see if you can find some of the disciples and see what they tell you about stealing the body.

DARIO: Right on boss. *(Exits.)*

ASHER: Hope they don't bring me any crazy stories of how tombs opened up this time or people being raised from the dead. I want facts.

Scene 2

(This scene can be held off to one side while the next scene is set up. Newsboy is holding an armful of rolled scrolls and calling the headlines.)

NEWSBOY: Read all about it. Jewish blasphemer crucified. Said He was the Son of God. Read all about it.

JOSEPH *(walks across stage talking)*: I know this story will be my big break. Let's see what could the headlines be for my story. Temple authorities puzzled. Disciples disappear with body.

Scene 3

(Temple offices, people are milling about, some hurry from one side of the stage to the other. Joseph enters, looks around for his friend and hurries over to Marcus.)

MARCUS: Figured you'd be here pretty soon.

JOSEPH: What's been happening?

MARCUS *(looks around furtively)*: You've got to keep me out of this.

JOSEPH: Sure, sure, I don't let on where I get my information.

MARCUS: The men who were guarding the tomb of Jesus came in a little while ago and said there was an earthquake. They didn't know how the stone in front of the tomb was moved either.

JOSEPH *(taking notes)*: The earthquake could have moved the stone in front of the tomb, couldn't it?

MARCUS: No. The guards said somebody, one person. *(Looks around furtively again.)* They said an angel moved it.

JOSEPH: Can't be done. *(Stops writing.)* One person couldn't move the stone and my boss won't believe an angel moved it.

MARCUS: Look, I could lose my job if they find out I'm talking to you about this. That's what they said, an angel.

JOSEPH: Okay, go on, what else?

MARCUS: The guard said they were like dead men. They couldn't move. This angel's appearance was so bright, like, *(pause)* like lightning they said. Some women came to the tomb then to anoint the body but the tomb was empty.

JOSEPH: Hmmn, likely story. Sounds like the guards had too much wine.

MARCUS: No! I saw them, they were scared. They hadn't been drinking.

JOSEPH: They could have fallen asleep and the disciples stole the body. Then the women could have been playing along, knowing all the time the body was gone. That would remove suspicion from the disciples. *(Scratches head.)*

MARCUS: I don't know. Things are pretty strange with the second earthquake and the only stone that was moved was in front of the tomb of Jesus.

JOSEPH: Is there anything else? What's all the excitement now?

MARCUS: My friend in the treasury *(Looks around again to see if anyone is watching.)* said that the High Priest asked for a large amount of currency. He had to take it to him, and the guards were still in the room. Looks to me like they are bribing the guards.

JOSEPH: Wow, what a story!

MARCUS: Remember, I'll deny I told you any of this.

JOSEPH: I'll tell my editor that my informant is reliable, but I won't expose you. *(Turns to leave.)*

MARCUS: Joseph, I'd go careful. It won't help to get all the chief priests mad. They can make life really miserable for you and your family.

JOSEPH *(absentmindedly)*: Right. Let's see, what would the head-line be? Guards bribed. Body gone. *(Exits.)*

Scene 4

(This scene could be held off to one side while the scene is changed.)

NEWSBOY *(has armful of scrolls)*: Read all about it. Jewish Blasphemer Dies, Temple Veil Torn Mysteriously. Read all about it.

Scene 5

(All the action takes place outside Mary's house. Jennifer knocks on door.)

MARY *(opens door)*: Yes, can I help you?

JENNIFER: I'm Jennifer from the *Jerusalem Journal,* and I wonder

70

if I might talk with you for a few minutes?

MARY: Why would you want to talk to me?

JENNIFER: You've been a follower of Jesus for some time, is that right?

MARY *(hesitant)*: Yes, I guess you might say that. Why do you ask?

JENNIFER: We're doing a follow-up story on the man Jesus and how His followers feel after the crucifixion.

MARY: I really don't want to talk about it.

JENNIFER: I realize this is a very difficult time. I'd just like a few words.

MARY: How would you feel? The greatest person who ever lived was killed. All He did was help people. He was compassionate. He would be so tired but would still help someone in need. *(Starts to cry.)* People treated Him very badly.

JENNIFER: I heard some unusual things happened this morning, could you tell me anything about that?

MARY *(rubs eyes)*: I still can't believe it. Because of the Sabbath, we couldn't anoint His body after they took Him off the cross, so we rose early today to go to the tomb. I was a little ahead of the other ladies and wondered who would be around to move the stone. We'd heard there were guards around, so we thought they might move it for us.

JENNIFER: What did you find when you got to the tomb?

MARY: At first I was glad the stone was moved, but then I realized the body was gone. I knew the disciples hadn't moved Him.

JENNIFER: How did you know it wasn't them?

MARY: They were so scared, only John was around during the crucifixion. They wouldn't have done it. Besides how could they with all the guards around?

JENNIFER: So you're saying the stone was moved, the body gone, and the disciples didn't do it? What else did you see?

MARY: I saw a man I thought was the gardener and I was crying, but I walked over to him and it was Jesus!

JENNIFER: What do you mean? Who?

MARY: It was Jesus. I asked the man where they put the body of Jesus, and all the man said was "Mary."

JENNIFER: What was unusual about that?

MARY: It was the way He said my name. I knew it was Jesus. He said I shouldn't hold onto Him because He hadn't gone to see His Father yet. I wasn't real sure what He meant. Then I ran back and told the disciples.

JENNIFER: What did He mean He hadn't gone to see His Father yet?

MARY: God is His Father. Jesus was dead and now He's alive and that's all I know. Jesus was dead and is alive!

(Mary closes the door and Jennifer walks across stage.)

JENNIFER: The boss will never believe this one. I'm not sure I do.

Scene 6

(This scene is the conference room at the paper. Joseph is pacing, Jude is slouched in a chair, Jennifer is going over her notes, and Dario is drumming his fingers on the table. After a pause, Asher bustles in.)

ASHER: Okay, what have we got?

JUDE: Good morning to you, Asher.

ASHER *(glances up and scowls)*: Okay, what do you have Jennifer?

JENNIFER: I talked to Mary, one of the followers of Jesus. She went to the tomb, found the stone moved away, the tomb was empty, and she said she saw and talked to Jesus.

ASHER: Cut out the supernatural part. Can't use any of it.

JENNIFER: But the guards were there all night so . . . how do you explain?

ASHER: We won't use it. Find a new recipe for lamb stew, Jennifer. Jude, what did you find?

JUDE: Well, I talked to the science editor. You asked him about the hours of darkness the other day and how it could have happened. . . .

ASHER: Yes, yes.

JUDE: He said it was dark because there was an absence of light.

ASHER: Brilliant.

JOSEPH: I've got the story, boss, can I tell you now?

ASHER: Later, later.

(Joseph acts disgusted, throws himself in the chair.)

JUDE: I did find out from Nicodemus there is no secret entrance into the garden tomb.

ASHER: Dario, what do you have?

DARIO: I couldn't find any of those disciples. They are really in hiding. I have a lead they're holed up in an upper room, and I'm going to follow up on that.

ASHER: Why don't you check on Nathan's missing lamb?

DARIO: What do you mean, check on a lamb with all this going on?

ASHER *(gives a withering look and Dario falls silent)*: Nathan's my good friend and his children's pet lamb is missing. I want you to go see him and find out the details.

JOSEPH: Now it's my turn. *(Joseph leans forward all excited.)* I went over to the temple as you said I should and found my informant over there. Things are crazy over there. Everybody is running around. The chief priest asked for a lot of money from the treasury. . . .

ASHER *(interrupts)*: Can't use it.

JOSEPH: My informant heard that the guards were being paid off.

ASHER: I said, we can't use it. I want you to find out about the ox in the ditch near Bethany.

JOSEPH: The greatest story of my career is breaking, and you won't even listen to me! Find out about an ox!

ASHER: Out. All of you get out and find some news. We have a paper to put out.

(All talk as they exit.)

JUDE: What's bothering him?

JENNIFER: Guess he doesn't like anything he doesn't understand.

DARIO: Who knows? Wonder if Nathan found his missing sheep. What's the headline for that? That should be worth a byline, right? *(Laughs.)*

JOSEPH: I know. The temple people got to him and he's scared to run the story. I knew it was true. This proves it. The temple said they would pull all their advertising if he said a word about what is going on. I know there is a story here and they can't stop me. *(Runs ahead of them offstage.)*

DARIO: Do you think that's the reason he backed off like that?

JUDE: Could be. The temple has a lot of pull. I've seen them squash other stories, although not quite like this. They're usually more subtle.

DARIO: I know one of the guards. We were on the same sport team. I might check that angle out.

JUDE: Go ahead, but Asher won't print it. You're wasting your time.

(Asher is alone, he jingles coins in his hand for a space of time. Then he hears a newsboy calling the new headline and he throws a coin across the room.)

NEWSBOY: Lamb Lives. Read all about it. Lamb Lives. Read all about it.

At this point other newsboys could go through audience and distribute scrolls with the plan of salvation.

The Great Cover-up

Matthew 27:62-66; 28:11-15

The first scene shows five soldiers guarding the tomb. During their discussions there are three "flashbacks." It ends with a scene at the temple where priests are trying to find some way to cover up the disappearance of Jesus' body. It is rather serious as the guards try to cope with what happened and begin to wonder about the man in the tomb.

This skit uses 17 men, though some could double in roles.

Characters
THADDEUS—Older, fiesty soldier.
GAIUS—Young, brash soldier.
TOBIAS—Officer of the guards, more formal.
LYSIAS—Cynical.
FELIX—A thinker, relaxed type.

Disciple Scene

PHILIP, ANDREW, MATTHEW

Garden Scene

JESUS, and three disciples

Guard Scene

Figure in white

Chief Priests Office

SCRIBE, CAIAPHAS, two other priests

Props

Everyone is dressed in Bible-times clothes. Also needed are a light bulb under sticks for an artificial fire, extra wood, book, desk, scrolls, little bags for money, and twelve baskets with bread.

Scene 1

(On the left side of the stage, show tomb and big stone—may be cut from cardboard which can be moved aside. In front are five guards around a fire. The right side of the stage is used for the other scenes or flashbacks.)

THADDEUS *(sarcastically, to Gaius):* I hope guarding a tomb isn't too strenuous for your first assignment.

GAIUS: No, I think I can handle it. Not too many people go around stealing bodies. Isn't this a strange duty?

TOBIAS: There must be some reason since Pilate okayed the request of the Jewish high priests. They think the disciples of Jesus will try to steal His body.

GAIUS: Why would they want to do that?

LYSIAS: These Jews have many weird ideas. Who knows?

FELIX: There were many strange happenings when Jesus was in town. He upset a lot of people from the high priests to Pilate.

GAIUS: All I've heard since I got here is about this Jesus. Who was He?

Thaddeus: Hey boy, put some fuel on the fire. *(Rubs hands together.)* Then we'll tell you a bedtime story.

(Gaius gets fuel and sits down with others around the fire.)

LYSIAS: First you have to realize these Jews are different. They believe in only one God and you wouldn't believe the set of rules and regulations they have. Some of these men sit all day working out everything they can and can't do. Why they even figure out how far a person can walk on the Sabbath. Ridiculous. *(Shakes head.)*

GAIUS: What did this have to do with Jesus?

LYSIAS: Jesus broke all their rules. He healed people on the Sabbath, and that's work. It's okay for a man to take a cow out of a hole but not to heal anyone.

76

GAIUS: This Jesus healed people?

FELIX: They said He was a miracle worker. He was supposed to have fed thousands of people with a handful of food.

LYSIAS: Not only that, there was food left over.

Scene 2

Disciples

(On the right side of stage, three disciples are talking. There are twelve baskets scattered around with bread in them.)

ANDREW: Look at all this food left over. *(Looks around and points to baskets.)*

PHILIP: You know, when Jesus asked me how we were going to feed everybody, I couldn't believe He was serious.

MATTHEW: I counted five thousand men, plus women and children. *(Finger to chin, contemplatively.)*

PHILIP: I thought Jesus would send the people away.

ANDREW: After Jesus sent us looking, I found a boy with his lunch and took him to the Master. I sure didn't know what good five small barley loaves and two fish would do.

MATTHEW: Mathematically there was no way to divide up those fish and loaves. Jesus thought of everything, even to arranging the men into groups of fifty to make it easier to go among them to pass out the food.

ANDREW: I was amazed how He took that boy's lunch, looked up, prayed to God, and broke the loaves and fish. He filled the baskets over and over. What a miracle!

PHILIP: Everyone had enough to eat and it sure tasted good.

MATTHEW *(counts baskets):* There are twelve baskets of food left.

(Philip reaches down and breaks off a chunk of bread.)

Scene 3

Soldiers

(Back to the campfire on the left side of stage.)

GAIUS: Jesus must have been a miracle worker to feed five thousand people and have twelve baskets of food left over. You'd think the priests would be happy to have someone like that around.

THADDEUS: Hey, boy, more fuel. *(Changes position.)*

(Gaius gets up and gets more wood and adds some to fire.)

THADDEUS: Not too much, we don't have to heat up all Jerusalem!

GAIUS: Sorry, sir. *(Puts the rest of the wood to the side.)* Tell me more about this Jesus. What else did He do?

FELIX: Well, many people were drawn to Him. He was treated like a king. One day people waved palm branches and threw their coats on the path in front of Him and His donkey.

LYSIAS: I would like to have seen the faces of the high priests while this was going on.

FELIX: The people shouted something about Hosanna to David's Son or something like that.

GAIUS *(gets up and paces back and forth):* If everyone liked Him, why would the priests have Him killed?

TOBIAS: What Jesus taught was in direct conflict with what the priests said. They couldn't have someone going around preaching against their system.

THADDEUS: The priests were afraid of losing their power.

LYSIAS: And their income.

FELIX: One of the ways of raising money was the sale of animals. A poor farmer comes into town without an animal and there is no other place where people can buy one. The priests can charge what they want; the farmer has no choice.

LYSIAS: It's a real money-maker. Or if someone brings in an animal, the priests say it isn't acceptable so the farmer has to buy one. Then the priests turn around and sell the poor man's lamb to the next person who comes along.

TOBIAS: Imagine how the priests felt when Jesus went into the temple and overturned the tables of the money changers. They didn't like it when Jesus said the temple was a den of robbers instead of a place of prayer.

LYSIAS: That really upset the priests. *(Laughs.)*

GAIUS: Wait a minute. Let me get this straight. Jesus did all this while the priests were there?

THADDEUS: That's right.

GAIUS: Sounds like a troublemaker to me.

LYSIAS: I don't blame Jesus. Those pompous old fools take advantage of the common people. They say one thing and do another. They had to get rid of Jesus.

TOBIAS: Jesus was too popular with the people, and they couldn't arrest Him when He taught at the temple.

FELIX: One of His own disciples played right into the hands of the priests.

THADDEUS: This unhappy disciple told the high priests when Jesus would be almost alone.

Scene 4

Garden

(Right side of stage, Jesus and three disciples are on stage.)

JESUS: Wait here while I pray. My soul is crushed with horror and sadness to the point of death. Stay awake with me. *(Jesus moves off a little.)*

(Peter, James and John sit down.)

JOHN: I've never seen Jesus so upset before.

JAMES: I'm tired. It has been a long day. *(Stretches and yawns.)*

PETER: So am I. I'm going to stretch out a little.

JESUS *(throws himself on the ground in agony):* My Father, if it is possible, let this cup be taken away from me. *(Pause.)* But I want Your will, not Mine. *(Pause, stands up and returns to the sleeping disciples.)* Peter, are you asleep?

PETER *(sits up and rubs his eyes):* I'm sorry, Jesus. I meant to stay awake.

JESUS: Couldn't you even stay awake with me for an hour? Keep alert and pray; otherwise, temptation will overpower you. I know your spirit is willing, but your body is weak. *(Walks away and kneels in prayer.)*

PETER: Yes, Lord. *(Shakes John and James.)* Hey John, James, wake up. We're suppose to pray.

(John and James stir around and sit up. Gradually the three of them fall asleep again.)

JESUS: My Father, take this cup from Me. Everything is possible for You. *(Pause.)* Yet not what I want but what You want. *(Pause. Jesus walks back to disciples who are sleeping again, leans over, and touches their shoulders.)* Wake up, can't you keep watch with me?

(Peter, James, and John all sit up again and once more gradually their heads bob as they doze off.)

JESUS: Dear Father, please remove this cup from Me. *(Pause.)* I want Your will, not Mine. *(Pause before He returns again to the disciples.)* Are you still sleeping? Enough! The hour has come.

(Peter, James, and John shake themselves awake.)

JESUS: Look! The Son of Man is betrayed into the hands of sinners. Rise! Let us go! Here comes my betrayer.

(Peter, James and John jump up. Peter grabs his sword.)

Scene 5

Guards

(Back to the left side of stage, Felix is coming back to the fire with fuel.)

TOBIAS: There was another reason they didn't want to arrest Him in the middle of a crowd. If Jesus had supernatural powers, they didn't want to look like fools in front of all the people.

THADDEUS: It must have been funny to see them take a whole company of men to arrest one man. The priests had another problem. They couldn't hold Him for seven days without a trial, and it was a very explosive situation with all the extra people in town.

GAIUS: Why did they have to hold Him for seven days?

LYSIAS: Another one of their silly rules.

FELIX: The priests were glad Judas had betrayed Jesus. To

make things look good, they had to go through the motions of a legal trial and the execution had to take place before sundown the next day.

LYSIAS *(stands up and laughs):* You should have seen them scurrying back and forth trying to figure out what to do. *(Pretends to run around like the priests.)* They broke all their own rules. They took Him to Annas first then brought Him to Caiaphas the high priest. The elders, scribes, and chief priest had gathered.

TOBIAS: It was a fake trial. *(Laughs.)* They had problems with the witnesses.

LYSIAS *(interrupts):* Yeah. They didn't have time to rehearse two people to tell the same story.

THADDEUS: One witness said Jesus would destroy the temple and raise it again in three days. That made them mad.

GAIUS: What was Jesus finally accused of?

TOBIAS: They asked Him if He was the Messiah, the Son of God. Jesus said, "I am." That was blasphemy to them.

GAIUS: Let me get this straight. The Jews held their secret meetings even though they couldn't put anyone to death without Rome's approval. Is that right?

THADDEUS: Right. The way I see it, time was short. They must have had somebody talking to Pilate that night. They had to know Pilate would go along with them and not insist on a full trial.

TOBIAS: That would explain Pilate's willingness to meet with the Jews outside his normal chambers.

GAIUS: Why would Pilate have to go outside his chambers?

FELIX: This whole business is pretty unusual. The Jews couldn't go into the regular chamber because that would "defile" them.

LYSIAS *(sarcastically):* They could plot to kill a man but they couldn't go into a certain room or they couldn't celebrate their religious holiday. They have some strange rules.

FELIX: Pilate thought he could satisfy the crowd if Jesus was beaten and taken out to the people. He tried to release Jesus, but the crowd shouted for Barabbas.

GAIUS: People are sure funny. In less than a week people went from singing and waving palm branches to wanting to kill Him. There was something else you said. Who is Barabbas and what does he have to do with all this?

FELIX: Well, it's the governor's custom at the feast to let the crowd chose to release a prisoner. Barabbas was the most notorious man he could think of. Pilate was sure the crowd would want Jesus released.

LYSIAS: These priests thought of everything. They had people planted among the crowd ready to shout, "Crucify Him." When a mob gets going, the rest of the people join in. Pilate washed his hands in front of the people to show he wasn't guilty of killing an innocent man. What a coward.

GAIUS: I'm beginning to feel sorry for this man, Jesus.

LYSIAS: It's a little late for Him now.

GAIUS: Couldn't His friends do anything?

THADDEUS: His followers weren't politically important and they all scattered when Jesus was arrested.

TOBIAS: Jesus was in no condition to carry His cross after all He'd been through. A soldier forced a bystander to carry the cross for Him.

FELIX: Unusual things happened that day. The sky went dark for three hours while He hung on the cross, the temple curtain was torn in two, tombs opened, and there was an earthquake.

GAIUS: That was scary. I was here when the earthquake happened.

TOBIAS (stands up and stretches): Oh, I'm tired of sitting. I'm glad the night is almost over.

FELIX: You know there was another strange thing. (Rubs chin.) I've never seen anyone die as quickly as Jesus did.

LYSIAS: A good thing since the Jews have another rule. The bodies of people crucified have to be removed and buried before the Sabbath.

GAIUS: How do you know all these things?

TOBIAS: After you live here a while you find out their strange customs.

(Stage grows dimmer, there's a thundering noise like a drum roll, lights flicker, and one bright light shines on a figure in white who moves the stone away from the tomb. The guards tremble and move in slow motion. They start to stand up but fall to ground.)

GAIUS: What happened?

TOBIAS: Did you see that? There was someone in white. His clothes were as bright as lightning. (Rubs eyes.)

THADDEUS: I thought I was imagining things. Look! It can't be! That huge stone is moved. It takes four men to move one that big.

FELIX: They shouldn't have killed Jesus.

LYSIAS: Did you feel the earth shake or was it my imagination?

GAIUS: Then it wasn't just me. I felt it too.

TOBIAS: Thaddeus, go look in the tomb.

THADDEUS: Me, sir? *(Visibly shaken.)*

TOBIAS: That's an order.

THADDEUS: Yes, sir. *(Thaddeus walks slowly over to the tomb, pauses, looks in, and dashes back.)* The body's gone.

FELIX: We're in big trouble.

LYSIAS: They'll never believe us.

GAIUS: Can we push the stone back in place?

TOBIAS: It wouldn't do any good. The Roman seal is broken.

FELIX: Let's leave Jerusalem now.

THADDEUS: They'll find us.

GAIUS: What are we going to do?

TOBIAS: We'd better report what happened.

THADDEUS: They won't believe us. They'll kill us, sir.

TOBIAS: We have to go report.

THADDEUS: If you go, we all have to go.

LYSIAS: Those sneaky priests can come up with some story.
(Guards all hurry off.)

Scene 6

Chief Priest's Office

(On the right side of the stage, Scribe is sitting at desk with a large book.)

TOBIAS: We need to see Caiaphas.

SCRIBE: Do you have an appointment? *(Starts to look in book.)* Of course it is too early in the morning. Would you like to make an appointment? It's going to be a busy day. I might be able to squeeze you in about . . .

TOBIAS: Be quick man. This concerns the matter of the tomb of Jesus you wanted crucified.
(Scribe scurries off. Caiaphas and other priests enter.)

CAIAPHAS: What's so important it can't wait until normal time?

TOBIAS *(stammers):* Ahh . . . Jesus' body is gone.

CAIAPHAS: What do you mean the body is gone? You fell asleep. I'll have you hung.

ALL GUARDS *(protest):* We were awake.

CAIAPHAS: Quiet!

TOBIAS: We were awake, sir.

THADDEUS: All of a sudden it got darker.

GAIUS: The earth shook.

LYSIAS: Then it got real bright. We saw a figure in white move the stone.

FELIX: It wasn't like anything I've ever seen. It was *(pause)* supernatural.

TOBIAS: Then everything was back to normal except the stone was moved.

CAIAPHAS: Did you see anyone remove the body?

(Guards shake heads no.)

CAIAPHAS *(confers with chief priests):* These men couldn't have made up such a preposterous story.

PRIEST 1: What are we going to do?

PRIEST 2: I knew something like this would happen.

PRIEST 1: The guards are really shaken.

CAIAPHAS *(turns to guards):* The ground shook?

TOBIAS *(as leader, he speaks):* The earth shook and at the same time there was lightning and someone in white moved the stone.

(The priests confer again. They continue talking while one leaves and comes back with bag of money. The guards are very nervous.)

CAIAPHAS *(takes money bag from other priest, turns to guards):* This is what you're to do. You're to say His disciples came during the night and stole the body while you slept.

TOBIAS: What happens if the Governor finds out about this?

CAIAPHAS: We'll satisfy him and keep you out of trouble. Take this and divide it up among you. Be sure you don't say anything to anyone about what really happened.

(Tobias and other guards exit and continue to talk after they move away from the priests.)

TOBIAS: Remember. We're to spread the word the disciples took the body.

FELIX: But we were awake all night. I know the man in the tomb was dead and I saw the seal put on the tomb. How can I lie about that?

TOBIAS: Felix, pay attention. All of our lives depend on obeying orders. Do you want to be killed?

FELIX *(doesn't answer question):* There's been something strange about this Jesus from the first I heard of Him.

GAIUS *(brashly proclaims):* I know what I saw.

TOBIAS *(hands him coins out of the bag):* Look, we have no choice. *(Gives coin to Thaddeus.)*

THADDEUS *(takes coin and looks at it):* I've got a wife and kids. I fell asleep while guarding the tomb.

GAIUS: Why do they want us to lie?

TOBIAS: We don't have to know. We have to cover up for the priests. We were on duty because of the priests. They want us to cover up, that's what we do!

GAIUS: If we don't go along, they'll . . .

TOBIAS: Right.

FELIX *(like he hadn't heard):* We watched the stone move.

(Lights fade.)

Antioch's Mission Board

Based on Acts 13

If Paul and Barnabas were members in your church what would your mission board require? What if Paul and Barnabas had to go before a mission board at the church in Antioch, could it have been like this?

This short skit is based on Acts 13 and needs eleven characters. It brings out the importance of missions at home and abroad and how everyone can be involved.

Characters

PRESIDENT HEBER—Sympathetic to missions and Paul and Barnabas.

SECRETARY TOBIAS—A prayer warrior.

ZEDERIAH—Afraid of possible persecution and the amount of money to be raised.

PHINNEAS—Believes in Paul and Barnabas.

LAGGAI—Wants to find a precedent.

TILEMON—Believes in training for missionaries and starting at a young age.

MOSEA—Supportive because he can't go himself.

JAHUM—Reluctant at first. He'd rather do missions from a distance.

AMMIHUD—Concerned about persecution if they are known as a sending church for missionaries.

SAUL/PAUL—Missionary candidate.

BARNABAS—Missionary candidate.

Props

A bag of scrolls, chairs, and a big table are needed. Cast wears Bible-times clothes.

ANNOUNCER: Most churches today have a mission board. They have goals, requirements, and by-laws. Before a missionary goes out, there are psychological tests to see if he is qualified for cross-cultural outreach. Length of term on the field is discussed and total amount of support to be paid is agreed upon. We are told in Acts 13:2, 3 "While they were worshiping the Lord and fasting, the Holy Spirit said, 'Set apart for me Barnabas and Saul for the work to which I have called them.' So after they had fasted and prayed, they placed their hands on them and sent them off" *(New International Version)*.

Scene 1

(Paul and Barnabas are waiting outside the mission board meeting room to give the board more details about their going out as missionaries.)

PAUL *(paces back and forth)*: Well, we're right on time to meet with the mission board. Do you have all the papers and certificates we need?

BARNABAS *(looks through a bag of scrolls)*: I have the transcripts of our schooling, how much support we can raise from our families and friends, and where we are going and for approximately how long.

PAUL: At least we know the language so we don't have to go to language school or learn how to prepare for cross-cultural shock. *(Stops in front of Barnabas.)* When you talked to President Heber, did he sound like he thought it was a good idea?

BARNABAS: President Heber has always been interested in spreading the gospel, but it's a rather new idea for the church to send out missionaries. It's never been done before.

PAUL: I hope they realize it isn't our financial needs we want but their approval and prayer support. We'll be faced with a lot of opposition.

BARNABAS: We'll soon find out. I hear someone coming for us now. *(Stands up.)*

TOBIAS: Good evening, Paul, Barnabas. *(Shakes hands with them.)* We're ready to have you speak to us now. We finished reading the minutes from our last meeting and are eager to hear what you have to say.

Scene 2

(The mission board members are seated around a table with scrolls in front of them. President Heber ushers Paul and Barnabas into the room.)

PRESIDENT HEBER *(to Paul and Barnabas)*: Here we are, gentlemen. We're glad you could join us today, Paul, whom some of you may know as Saul, and Barnabas. The board is aware of your proposal and we're eager to hear what you have to say.

PAUL: Since you've seen our proposal, I won't go into a lot of preliminary details. As believers, we are to tell others the good news of Jesus Christ. If you remember, during my conversion experience, Ananias was told to come to me. He said I was God's chosen instrument to carry the gospel to the Gentiles and their kings and before our own people. I believe the time has come to make a definite move into the Gentile world. What Barnabas and I desire is the mission board's prayer support and blessing as we make our journey. I'd like to show you our proposed itinerary which, of course, may vary depending on our acceptance in the various cities.

(Barnabas hands Paul the map scroll. Paul unrolls it and lays it on the table. The men stand up and gather around so they can see. Paul points to spot on scroll.)

PAUL: We'd leave from Seleucia and go to the island of Cyprus first. We land at Salamis on this end of the island and go to the other end at Paphos where we'll take a ship to Perga to the mainland. Then we'd head up to Pisidian Antioch and perhaps to Lystra or Derbe. A lot of this will, of course, depend on our reception in each area. Since you've seen our proposal, perhaps it would be better to answer any questions you have at this time.

LAGGAI: Do you really think this is a good idea? To my knowledge I don't remember another church sending out missionaries. How do we know what to do?

PAUL: If we don't go, how will the people know about Christ? Jesus said we were to go into all the world.

MOSEA: How long do you expect to be gone?

BARNABAS: A lot of that depends on how we are received. We want to establish other churches. We need to find good people to begin their own churches.

PHINNEAS: Are you looking at months or years?

PAUL: We plan on being gone around a year. It's hard to say at this point.

(The mission board members all sit down.)

ZEDERIAH: That could cost a lot of money. Do we know how much we have in our mission account?

LAGGAI: We don't have a precedent to know how much we should allot for sending out missionaries.

TILEMON: Don't you think we could get the people really excited and have some extra collections?

PAUL: I can always make a few tents if we need to pay our expenses. Our biggest concern isn't financial.

PHINNEAS: Then the work would take longer because you'd have to work all day and only preach at night and on the weekends.

TILEMON: I think we should try to raise all the money they need so they can devote full time to spreading the gospel.

(A pause with no questions.)

PRESIDENT HEBER: Are there other questions any of you want to ask Paul or Barnabas? *(He looks around and no one responds.)* If there isn't, then they may be excused and we will continue in our deliberations.

AMMIHUD: President Heber, I have a question for Paul. Christians are already being imprisoned or killed for their faith. Don't you think if you go out as missionaries, you'll be persecuted? Is this a good time to begin a new ministry?

PAUL: I don't think we really have any other choice. Jesus gave us a mandate to go into all the world to preach the gospel. I feel very strongly this is something we are called to do no matter what happens to us as individuals.

LAGGAI: Do you know of any other churches that have sent out missionaries?

PAUL: Well, Philip and Peter traveled around the country quite a bit. Peter was in Joppa, Caesarea and many other places. I'm sure the church in Jerusalem helped with his needs and his family.

PRESIDENT HEBER: Are there any more questions? *(Pause.)* If not, we thank you for coming a second time to meet with our board and to give us more details.

BARNABAS *(stands)*: If there are any other questions, we will be waiting outside, so you can call us back in. Thank you for allowing us to present our needs.

(Paul and Barnabas shake hands with everyone.)

PRESIDENT HEBER: Thank you, Paul, Barnabas. We'll discuss the matter further and call you.

(Paul and Barnabas exit.)

PRESIDENT HEBER: Well, gentlemen we've heard the plan of Paul and Barnabas. It's up to us if we want to support them and, if so, by how much. Let's have some discussion on this matter.

AMMIHUD: I don't know if our church should make such a commitment now and call a lot of attention to ourselves. Look at the church in Jerusalem and the persecution it's undergone.

TOBIAS: That's true, but Paul is right. Jesus said we're to take the good news to all the world.

AMMIHUD: Well, because of the persecution many believers have been scattered and they'll tell others.

PHINNEAS: That's true but we need to be actively involved. I think it's great Paul and Barnabas are willing to go. The least we can do is support them in any way possible.

MOSEA: I agree with Phinneas. I can't leave my bagel bakery to go since I have such a large family to support, but I'm sure happy to help Paul and Barnabas any way I can.

ZEDERIAH: I'd feel better about it if we knew how much indebtedness we are talking about. The monthly support they are asking for is certainly reasonable, but he can't even guess how long this is going to go on. This might go on for years and years.

JAHUM: What if we wrote down some of the sayings of Jesus and made a scroll and sent it out next time? That would be cheaper. We could get a mailing list from each of the different cities he mentioned.

PRESIDENT HEBER: Not everybody knows how to read. How did you find out about Jesus and salvation? Did you read it in a scroll or did someone tell you? The best way is to send a person to explain.

JAHUM: That's true. Someone told me and he was there to answer my questions.

AMMIHUD: I think we're forgetting something. What about all the people in our own town who haven't heard about Jesus.

Shouldn't we be telling them first before we send people all over the world?

TOBIAS: That's something we should be doing. We can do that while Paul and Barnabas go farther afield.

LAGGAI: I don't know. I wish there was some precedent we could refer to.

PRESIDENT HEBER: I think we should be trying to think of ways to encourage Paul and Barnabas rather than thinking of reasons we shouldn't help them.

TOBIAS: I agree. What can we do?

MOSEA: Our church could be a real support team. We could write letters so they don't get discouraged and send packages to them.

TOBIAS: We could pray for them. I'd be willing to set up a prayer chain. When the board hears from Paul, I'll let everyone know his prayer needs.

PRESIDENT HEBER: This is what I like, a positive way to look at the problem.

ZEDERIAH: How about letting other churches help us in their support?

TOBIAS: Wouldn't it be better if our church supported Paul and Barnabas and other churches sent out other missionaries? Soon all the world would have heard the gospel.

TILEMON: What about starting to train other missionaries in our church?

JAHUM: We could begin with children. They could start by reading biographies of famous missionaries.

MOSEA: I hope you're not thinking about Jonah. He wasn't one of the best examples of a missionary. (Laughs.)

TOBIAS: We could have mission conferences to get the rest of our church body excited.

TILEMON: This could include the children.

JAHUM: I'd be willing to organize a children's mission conference.

LAGGAI: It's never been done before to my knowledge.

MOSEA: We can be the first. If we make mistakes, we'll know better the next time.

ZEDERIAH: Maybe we could have a few events like a camel wash or something to help raise money to support them.

LAGGAI: Well, I guess somebody has to be first to do something. I wish it wasn't us, but let's do the best we can.

JAHUM: After Paul gets back and finds out what works, we could write up some tracts to hand out.

PRESIDENT HEBER: It sounds like we may be ready for a vote. All in favor of supporting Paul and Barnabas going out as missionaries from our church say aye. *(The men all agree.)* Those opposed, nay. The aye's have it gentlemen. We'll send Paul and Barnabas with our full approval and support.

TOBIAS: Shall I find them and tell them the good news?

PRESIDENT HEBER: Yes, bring them back in. We want their ideas on the best way to present this to the congregation at our next service.

Runaway

Book of Philemon

This short skit is based on the small book of Philemon and uses three characters, Onesimus, Dario and Philemon. Onesimus returns with a letter from Paul and stops first to greet another slave. The two of them go in to see Philemon and there the fate of Onesimus is decided. Philemon has a legal right to kill his slave but both he and Onesimus are Christians. What do you think happened? The main point in this skit is forgiveness.

Characters

DARIO—A slave to Philemon.

ONESIMUS—A runaway slave.

PHILEMON—Slaveowner, Christian, friend of Paul's, holds church services in his home.

Props

Actors all dress in Bible-times clothes. Other props are plants, a container for weeds, a writing desk, and a scroll.

Scene 1

(The setting is a garden area outside the home of Philemon. The slave, Dario, is kneeling and pulling weeds.)

ONESIMUS *(enters)*: Greetings, Dario.

DARIO *(quickly turns, speaks softly and looks around)*: Onesimus, is that really you?

ONESIMUS: Yes it is. I've come back to see Philemon and be his slave again.

DARIO: What? You know the punishment for a runaway slave. *(Looks around again.)* He'll kill you or flog you at least. Besides running away, I heard you stole from our Master. I wouldn't have come back if I were you.

ONESIMUS: So much has happened. I had to come back.

DARIO: I wouldn't want to be in your sandals.

ONESIMUS: There's something I want to tell you before I see Philemon. I'll kneel down and help you with the garden work and our talking won't be so noticeable.

(They both stoop and work among the plants.)

DARIO: Tell me what you did. Where did you go?

ONESIMUS: I was scared when I left. I took untraveled paths, mostly at night. After I got to Colossae I mingled with the crowds. While I was in the city, I met Paul, a Christian and a friend of our master, Philemon.

DARIO: Let's move over here. Right now we're trying to get everything ready for the church meeting tomorrow. *(He moves to the right and Onesimus follows him.)* Go on, then what?

ONESIMUS *(tugs at a weed and reaches for another one)*: I talked a lot with Paul. He told me Christians believe Jesus is the Son of God who came to earth. He told me many things Jesus said and how He performed many miracles, including healing people.

DARIO: Didn't the Jews convince Herod to crucify Him? It seems I remember hearing something about that and then His disciples said the tomb was empty.

ONESIMUS: That's right, Dario. Paul explained how Jesus came to die for the sins of all people. I didn't realize there is only one way to be in the right relationship with God.

DARIO: Which god are you talking about?

ONESIMUS: The only real God there is. Jehovah God, the God of the Jews.

DARIO: You mean Philemon's God? What did you have to do?

ONESIMUS: Everyone can be a Christian. You must believe Jesus is the Son of God and that He died for your sins. You ask Him to come into your life and you follow Him.

DARIO: I know that Philemon talks to us slaves once in a while about his God but I haven't paid much attention. What's a sin?

ONESIMUS: If we think of God as a lawgiver, it would be anything that goes against God's revealed nature or keeps us away from closeness to God. God forgave all my sins and things started to change in my life. I knew that the right thing to do was to come back and make things right with Philemon.

DARIO: This must be some God to bring you back. If you live, I want to hear more about this God of yours.

ONESIMUS: I'm sure we'll have a chance to talk later. I'd better see

Philemon now. Is he in his office as usual at this time of day?

DARIO: As far as I know. I'll go with you.

(Dario and Onesimus exit.)

Scene 2

(Philemon is sitting behind his writing desk.)

DARIO: Master, Onesimus is back.

PHILEMON *(jumps up)*: Get him in here.

(Dario and Onesimus enter.)

PHILEMON *(strides over to stand nose to nose with Onesimus)*: Wait outside Dario. Stay close. Don't let him past you.

DARIO: Yes, Master Philemon. *(Exits.)*

PHILEMON: So my trusted slave has come back. Did you come to steal more from me? Were you afraid I'd find you anyhow, so you came crawling back? *(Strokes his chin or beard and walks away.)*

ONESIMUS *(says quietly, looks down)*: Lord, help me to do and say what You want me to say. You are the One who showed me I should come back.

PHILEMON *(walks back close to Onesimus)*: Well, what do you have to say for yourself?

ONESIMUS: I know what I did was wrong. I've come back to be your obedient slave.

PHILEMON *(demanding, angry tone)*: Now tell me how you realized what you did was wrong. *(Backs up and crosses his arms.)*

ONESIMUS *(quietly)*: I became a Christian.

PHILEMON: What did you say?

ONESIMUS *(louder)*: I said I became a Christian.

PHILEMON: As your master, I have the authority to kill you if I want. You stole and ran away from me. *(Talks louder.)* Now you come in here claiming to be a Christian because you think that will please me. It won't work! Dario, come get this useless . . .

(Dario enters and waits for instructions.)

ONESIMUS: Please hear me, sir. It's because I became a follower of Christ I came back. I was taught slaves should obey their masters.

PHILEMON *(sneers)*: And just who was the Christian who taught you this?

ONESIMUS: Paul.

PHILEMON: Whom did you say?

ONESIMUS: Paul, the apostle, who is in chains in Colossae. I have a letter from him for you. *(He reaches inside his tunic and pulls out the scroll and hands it to Philemon.)*

PHILEMON *(acts surprised and takes scroll)*: Wait outside, Dario. *(Dario exits.)*

PHILEMON *(unrolls the scroll and reads part of it aloud, he relaxes)*: Your love has given me great joy and encouragement. *(Paces back and forth as he reads the letter.)* Yet I appeal to you for my son Onesimus who became my son while I was in chains. *(Questioning tone.)* Before he was useless to you, but now he has become useful both to you and to me. *(Stops and looks at Onesimus.)* So Paul considered you like his son. He would liked to have kept you with him. *(Finishes reading the scroll and taps the rolled up scroll on his left hand, stops in front of Onesimus to look at him and then resumes his pacing.)*
(Onesimus shifts his weight.)

PHILEMON *(unrolls the scroll, reads it once more)*: He's even willing to pay me back what you stole from me. *(Lays the scroll on his desk.)* You realize my rights as your slaveowner? I could kill you or at the least flog you.

ONESIMUS: Yes, Master Philemon. I deserve it.

PHILEMON *(paces a little more)*: Tell me more about Paul.

ONESIMUS: I remember how Paul looked when he dictated his letters. He writes so many letters and spends so much time in prayer even though he is constantly chained to a guard. *(Shakes his head.)* One of the latest guards seems really disinterested in learning about Christ, but if he's around Paul very much, even he will be touched by Paul's life-style.

PHILEMON: This is some letter he wrote me. He thinks I should welcome you as I would welcome him, even though you have wronged me. Paul certainly has a way of writing. What else can I do with such a recommendation? Welcome, brother. *(Hugs Onesimus.)*

NEW VILLAGE CONGREGATIONAL CHURCH
WILDWOOD ROAD (OFF ELLIOT AVE.)
P. O. BOX 191
LAKE GROVE, NEW YORK 11755